# A Part of the Ribbon

## a time travel adventure
## through the history of Korea

# A Part of the Ribbon
## a time travel adventure
## through the history of Korea

**Ruth S. Hunter**
**Debra M. Fritsch**

**Turtle Press**
**Hartford**

ISBN 1-880336-11-1
Printed in the U.S.A.

Library of Congress  Card Catalog Number 96-61175

Interior Illustrations by Ken Cotrona
Cover Illustration by Chris Nye
Photographs by Tom Pearce

*To write to the authors or to order additional copies:*
Turtle Press
PO Box 290206
Wethersfield CT 06129-0206
1-800-778-8785

# A Message from the Authors

Special thanks to Wayne Patterson, Tom Pearce, Patrick Petitjean, Yvonne Murnane, Cynthia Kim, Chris Nye and Ken Cotrona.

Thanks to my family: Bill, Theresa, Justin and Oriana for their constant encouragement and support and for all the fun

*Ruth S. Hunter*

I want to thank my family for their love, support, and encouragement on this project. Thanks, Jim, Kristin and

*Debra J. Fritsch*

# Note to Readers

As you travel through Korean history in *A Part of the Ribbon*, you will encounter many new words in the Korean language. To help you understand what the characters are experiencing, each of these words is included in the glossary at the back of the book. The first time a new word appears it will be in *italics* to remind you to look it up in the glossary. Some words are pronounced differently than they are spelled - these words have a pronunciation key with their definition.

# 1
## The Dojang

A dusting of fresh snow framed the *dojang's* storefront window. Inside, beads of moisture and threads of steam fogged the glass and the royal blue letters outlining the studio's name.

From the front of the large workout room, *taekwondo Sabum* Paul Meyer, fifth degree black belt and senior sparring champion, barked a command, "*Joochoom sogi!*"

Lines of alert students wearing white uniforms and bright crayon-colored belts immediately stepped left into low horse stances and threw out punches with their right fists. Sharp *kihaps* exploded from their mouths. All, that is, except for Jeffrey and Charlotte, two wide-eyed, white belts standing in the back line.

Thirteen-year old Jeffrey, skinny and tall for his age, quickly brushed his reddish blond hair off his forehead. He eagerly rolled his hand into a fist and punched.

Charlotte, who always gave her age as six and three-quarters, skeptically watched her brother Jeffrey. She frowned. The dark blonde pony tail perched on top of her head cascaded like a fountain, forming a fringe just above her soft brown eyes.

Charlotte halfheartedly stepped to the side and punched. Her attention wavered. Delicate wisps of fringe tickled her dark eyebrows as she scanned the line. Next to Jeffrey towered a plump, white haired man with a mustache and bright blue eyes. Further down the line, a four-year old, tow-headed boy rocked absentmindedly in a loose horse stance while his toes played with a piece of lint on the gray carpet.

Charlotte missed *Sabumnim*'s order to punch while she observed the other students. They were grouped by belt color, not by age or size. Charlotte counted four black belts in the front row.

"History is a ribbon connecting the past and its people to the present," forty-five year old Sabumnim said. He directed his comments to Charlotte who looked first at the ceiling and then at him. "Even our punches and kicks are the result of hundreds of years of trial and error."

Sabumnim's dark graying curls bobbed as he paced between the lines. "*Shijak!*"

Students pulled their right hands back to their belts and thrust out their left fists.

Sabumnim's observant blue eyes focused on Jeffrey's sharp elbows rising like chicken wings each time he punched.

"Feel your elbows brush your side as you pull your fist back to your belt," Sabumnim corrected.

Jeffrey pulled his elbows in.

"Shijak!"

8

This time the punch flew out with snap and power. Jeffrey grinned.

"Good job."

"You do it, Charlotte," Jeffrey whispered.

"When I'm ready!" Charlotte looked at her feet and pointed her toes forward. Then, making a fist, she punched.

"Good. Now bring the other hand back to your belt." Sabumnim showed her what he meant.

She sighed. Loudly.

Sabumnim walked around the room straightening wrists and redirecting punches of other students. "Widen your stances, bend your knees. The *Hwarangdo* used many of these techniques over 1350 years ago. What does Hwarangdo mean? Susan?"

"Way of the flowering youth, Sir," a perky, red-headed teenager said.

"Form a line against the back wall! Offensive techniques across the floor at your own pace. White belts, punches only across the floor."

Jeffrey stood between Charlotte and a tall, intense, middle-aged woman wearing a red belt. Her glossy black curls were gathered back into a tight bun; her glasses balanced near the tip of her nose.

Jeffrey glanced briefly at the older woman and with greater interest at the athletic, muscular twenty-four year old man wearing a green belt who stood next to Charlotte.

The red belt caught Jeffrey's rapid dismissal of her. Her lips quirked into a quick smile before she focused on a point on the wall ahead of her.

"Shijak!"

Everyone moved. Jeffrey and Charlotte stepped forward and punched, their heads bobbing with each movement. Out of the corner of his eye, Jeffrey watched the green belt do a double punch and a knife hand. Jeffrey grinned and focused forward just in time to see the red belt complete a low and high side kick followed by a knife hand and reverse punch.

Jeffrey punched again. The red belt led with a jumping front kick followed by a round house and spun into a back fist. Jeffrey's mouth dropped open.

The woman bit her cheek, and a glint of satisfaction glowed in her dark brown eyes.

"Who do we judge ourselves against?" Sabumnim asked Jeffrey.

Jeffrey gulped. "The best in the class, Sir?"

Sabumnim pointed to the red belt.

"Ourselves, Sir," she said. "We always try to improve what we can do."

"Good. Line up."

Students found their original positions in the rows. Sabumnim nodded to the woman, the highest ranking red belt in class.

"Face the instructor," she said, ending class. "*Charyut*." The students snapped to attention and placed their open hands at their sides over their belts. "*Kyungye*." They brought their fists forward and bowed. Jeffrey put his hands over his white belt and did the same.

Laughing and talking, the students disbanded.

Charlotte turned her head sharply to watch the other students. The ends of her ponytail bounced. She turned back to Jeffrey and put her hands on her hips, tiny elbows sticking straight out. "I don't know about this stuff, Jeffrey."

"Ssh!"

With a few quick strides, Sabumnim joined Jeffrey and Charlotte. "Keeping your elbows in really helped your punches."

"I liked the power of the punches. But the kicks!" Jeffrey, wild with energy, leapt into the air. His long, thin arms and legs flew every which way while he did his best impression of a jumping front kick and landed squarely on his backside. Color rose in his cheeks, clashing with his freckles.

"I guess I have to practice that one." He stood awkwardly and straightened his uniform. Crossing his arms defensively, he blurted, "I can understand practicing the kicks, but I don't understand why we have to know about history and people who have been dead forever."

"I once wondered the same thing," Sabumnim said.

The small, tow-headed boy tugged at Sabumnim's sleeve.

"Oh, yes, your glasses." Sabumnim removed them from the trophy shelf. "Here you go, Brian. See you on Wednesday." Smiling, Sabumnim turned back to Jeffrey and Charlotte.

"You had questions?"

Jeffrey studied Sabumnim's threadbare black belt.

Charlotte stopped fidgeting and listened closely.

"All learning begins with questions."

"Well, I have a ton of them, Sir. Where do I begin?" Several black belts and red belts re-entered the room to take advantage of the open workout time.

"Let's move out of their way. Over here."

Sabumnim motioned to the children to follow him. "Each person is different. For some, the answers are in the journey."

"The journey?" Jeffrey bounced on his toes.

At once, the room grew silent and still. The other students blurred into the background. Long, puffy strands of mist dropped from the ceiling and rose from the floor becoming thicker and thicker, totally engulfing them. They stood alone in a pale blue netherland. A wide, vibrantly blue silk ribbon rippled near their ankles.

"Come travel on the ribbon of time and you will understand how history affects each of us," Sabumnim said.

Jeffrey took Charlotte aside. "What an opportunity!" He shivered with excitement.

"Jeffrey, this is crazy!" Charlotte shook his arm. "We'll miss our ride home."

The dojang's round clock flew out of the blue mist, growing from its normal size to a sphere taller and wider than Sabumnim. It vibrated gently in the fog, but its black hands stood still. Three pairs of shoes floated in a circle around the clock.

"On our journey, even though we'll travel through 2,000 years, we'll be gone only a few moments. Ribbon time is different from our time," Sabumnim said.

Jeffrey's eyes gleamed. "I'm not going to miss this! I'm going." He nodded at Sabumnim.

"Then put on your shoes," Sabumnim said.

Charlotte hesitated only a moment. "If you go, I go!"

She jumped and swiped at her shoes floating above the clock. She missed. They floated lower, and she caught them.

"All together, then. On the count of three, step on the ribbon. Uh one, and uh two, and uh three!"

Sabumnim laughed at Jeffrey's dumfounded expression. "I'll explain sometime."

Together, the three stepped on the blue ribbon of time and vanished in the mist.

# 2
# Ancient Korea

When the mist cleared, Charlotte and Jeffrey sat on a roof thatched with bark and tied together with straw ropes. Charlotte inhaled the cool, fresh mountain air and shivered. She pulled her *dobok* tighter around her small body.

A white-bellied black woodpecker, clasping the side of an evergreen's trunk, stopped pecking to size up the intruders. Beautiful rainbow feathered birds trilled from their dark green perches.

Charlotte reached down the wide sleeve of her dobok and dislodged a piece of ragged bark. She shook it at Jeffrey. "What have you gotten us into? And where is Sabumnim?"

"Ouch!" Sabumnim moaned. "I'm down here."

Jeffrey and Charlotte crawled to a large, rough edged hole in the roof. Charlotte tried not to touch the coarse bark with her soft hands.

"Come on, Charlotte. It's nothing!" Jeffrey jeered. He crawled forward. "Ow!" He picked at his palm and yanked out a large splinter.

"Nothin'! Hmmph!" Charlotte snorted.

Reaching the hole, they peeked over the edge. Sabumnim lay sprawled in a stone lined pit dug in the dirt floor, dust settling around him from the force of his landing.

"I forgot how difficult ribbon travel can be!" Sabumnim got to his feet and dusted himself off, wincing slightly whenever he hit a tender spot.

"Is this a house?" Jeffrey grabbed the free end of a section of bark and swung clumsily through the opening.

"Not only is this a house, I landed in the kitchen's cooking area, right in the center of the room. I fell through the chimney hole." Sabumnim picked up a stone from the stove built into the hole in the floor. "Luckily no one's cooking right now."

The only light in the musty room came in through the door and the widened chimney hole in the roof. The dimness lent a sense of mystery to the room and its textured walls.

Intrigued, Jeffrey ran his fingers over the surface. "Look at this! The walls are made of logs and dirt and covered with vines. And part of the house is definitely underground!" He wandered around the small room.

"Ow!" Jeffrey tripped over a piece of pottery sticking out of the earth.

Sabumnim knelt to look at the pottery. He brushed aside some of the dirt. "It's a clay pot. They stored their grains in these pots under the ground in the kitchen."

15

Charlotte peered at them through the hole and waved. Sabumnim motioned her to meet them outside.

"We're in the mountains of Korea and it's almost 2,000 years ago. These are country people." Sabumnim walked to the door. "They built with whatever they could find. Farmers in the lowlands covered their roofs with thatched rice straw."

Charlotte laid on the roof and looked in through the open doorway, her head upside-down. "If houses are made of mud, do they melt when it rains?"

"Rarely. The sloping roofs provide protection. They're not like the houses back home." Sabumnim ducked to miss her head.

Instead of stooping, Jeffrey batted Charlotte's ponytail.

"Hey!" She pulled back onto the roof and stood up, arms akimbo. "How am I supposed to get down?"

"Do what I did," Jeffrey said. "Grab the bark and swing."

Charlotte hesitated only a moment. She took a deep breath and laid on her stomach. She wrapped her fingers around a section of bark, inched backwards to the roof's edge and dropped about five feet to the ground.

Charlotte tilted her chin high in the air. "Now you can't say I can't do what you do."

"Sure, Sis." Jeffrey patted her on the head.

Charlotte swiped at his hand.

"At this time," Sabumnim interrupted. "Korea is called *Choson* which means Land of the Morning Calm."

They heard a low growl. The underbrush rustled, branches splintered and cracked, and small animals scattered.

"Don't move." Sabumnim stood perfectly still.

A brown bear, the size of a minivan, plowed through the woods and onto the path. A necklace of weeds and garlic bulbs hung around her neck. She spied the travelers and paused; her small, coal black eyes freezing the travelers to their spots.

The bear sniffed Jeffrey; her thick fur bristled. She stood upright and roared. The air vibrated with the powerful sound. The bear dropped to all fours. With a slight shake of her head, she dismissed the travelers, plodded up the path and disappeared.

"Well, what do you know? I didn't realize we'd gone back so far in time," Sabumnim said.

"This way." Sabumnim started off, but Charlotte and Jeffrey stood rooted. Jeffrey's mouth hung open, and he pointed up the path. He tried to speak. "Bu, but. . ."

Sabumnim returned. He waved his hand in front of Jeffrey's face. "It's okay, you two! That was the famous bear of the legend." The children stopped watching the path and stared curiously at Sabumnim. He grinned.

"Once, long ago, high in these mountains a bear and tiger were given the chance to become human. They had to eat garlic and mugwort — those were the weeds the bear carried — and stay in a dark cave for one hundred days. The tiger got restless and left, but the bear stayed and turned into a beautiful woman. Later, she bore a son, *Dangun,* and in 2333 B.C., he became the legendary founder of Korea."

"Why couldn't we just see her when she was the beautiful woman?" Charlotte asked.

"Good question," Jeffrey said. He was much more relaxed now that the bear was gone.

They followed the ribbon to the brink of a cliff located high over the sea and countryside. Korea stretched before them, a lovely, mountainous peninsula crisscrossed with streams and rivers and surrounded on three sides by water.

"See the roads leading up and down the mountains and flat lands?" Sabumnim asked.

"Why are they so crooked?" Charlotte shaded her eyes from the bright morning sun and squinted.

"Because the people of this time believed that good and evil spirits lived in everything."

"Even rocks and trees?"

"In everything. The Shamin believed evil spirits could only move in straight lines. So by building crooked roads, people were safe to travel."

"Must have taken them a lot longer to get places," Jeffrey said. "The shortest distance between two points is a straight line." His voice rose in an imitation of his math teacher.

"They felt it was worth it. The spirits played a big part in their lives." Sabumnim stepped around rocks piled carefully at the beginning of a path leading higher into the mountains. "Another strong influence in their lives were the kings and kingdoms of Choson. Long ago, Choson was divided into four kingdoms.

"Over there to the south is *Shilla.*" He pointed to the bottom tip of Korea. "It's the oldest and the tiniest kingdom. See the mark on the ribbon? It's 57 B.C."

The ribbon lay passively on the ground and ran for hundreds of miles over plateaus, mountains, and valleys to the sea. The date 57 B.C. was stamped boldly in the fabric; other dates further along the ribbon were not legible.

"What about the southern land on the other side of the mountains? Is that Shilla too?" Jeffrey waved his hand in that direction.

"No, that's *Baekje*. The ribbon is marked 18 B.C. It's the youngest kingdom. In between Baekje and Shilla is *Kaya*, the tiny, forgotten kingdom. It was founded in 42 A.D."

As Sabumnim stated each year, the dates on the ribbon surfaced.

"To the north is *Koguryo,* the largest kingdom. It's marked at 37 B.C."

"Korea's not very big," Charlotte said, a surprised look on her face.

"That's right," Sabumnim said. "Even together the four kingdoms are much smaller than their neighboring countries of China or Siberia. And it's only a short trip across the sea to Japan.

"Korea's four kingdoms often fought against the Chinese. And later, the kingdoms fought each other for almost seven hundred years."

"Seven hundred years!" Charlotte blurted. "That's a long time."

"Can't we just tell them who won?" Jeffrey leaned over the edge of the cliff for a better view. His toes slipped, and he wobbled.

Sabumnim grabbed Jeffrey's belt and yanked him back. "I'm afraid not. This is their history. Later, we can come back and meet Shilla's Hwarangdo youth group."

"Why not now?"

"Because I want you to see how history builds, one step at a time. Step on the ribbon. We need to go to China to the Shaolin Temple in the early sixth century."

# 3

## Shaolin Temple

Jeffrey landed hard, his feet dangling in air. He opened his green eyes and gaped at a golden throne's massive back rising high over his head. The throne was ornately engraved with lotus leaves, two fish and a parasol. At the right of the throne, Jeffrey saw a bell topped by an eight-spoked wheel.

The room was enormous. Stark red columns of pine supported the high, raftered ceiling.

In the center, six monks sat cross-legged on the wooden floor, their eyes closed in meditation. Their backs were straight and their hands lay folded in their laps. Three faced Jeffrey's side of the room, and three faced Sabumnim and Charlotte on the other half of the room. The monks paid no attention to the newcomers.

Sabumnim and Charlotte stood and gazed silently at a huge, gold statue sitting cross-legged. The statue had long ear lobes and wore a robe gracefully draped over his shoulder. His head appeared to be covered by twists of tightly curled hair. Freshly cut flowers bloomed from the large vases on either side of the statue.

"That's Buddha. I studied about him last year in school." Jeffrey spoke in a whisper which carried to the far corners of the room. "He was a prince in the royal family of India."

Jeffrey slid off the throne and walked over to Sabumnim and Charlotte.

The monks still ignored the visitors.

"Buddha chose to teach his beliefs to his people and live among them instead of living lavishly as their ruler," Sabumnim said. "Many devoted their lives to studying his teachings and became monks.

"The Buddhist monks prayed for long periods of time, and found they needed to develop stamina. They learned the martial arts to gain control of their minds and bodies."

Loud shouts erupted outside.

"What's that?" Jeffrey ran to the temple's thick, wooden, red door. Lifting the iron bar, he pushed the door open.

Six pairs of sandals on the stairs pointed toward the temple. Jeffrey glanced quickly back into the room at the nearest monk, sitting calmly amid the confusion. Bare toes peeked from under his long robe.

Again the shouts came. "Look at all this!" Jeffrey said.

Granite walled buildings, some roofed with gray tiles and some with tan colored thatch, lined an enclosed courtyard. Graceful gardens created islands of peace among the stone paths leading to the center courtyard.

Fleecy clouds drifted across the deep blue of the sky, seemingly pushed along by the babble raised by the crowd in the courtyard.

Bald-headed monks dressed in sand colored, long robes taught lessons. A monk, who was missing several teeth, held a fly whisk in his bird-like fingers. The fly whisk's long strands were made with hair from a deer's tail. After listening to what a young boy had to say, the monk flicked the whisk around the boy's head.

"Maybe this will brush away your barriers to true enlightenment," he said.

Black-haired parents watched their sons study and perform. Some parents wore short, cream colored jackets and wide trousers and others dressed in elaborate red, yellow, blue or green silk garments decorated with borders and long drooping sleeves. The light yellowish-brown skin tones of the people ranged from the paler tones of those who spent most of their time inside to the darker tones of outdoor workers. Many of the young children were sunburned.

At the far end of the courtyard near the massive wooden doors stood a bald, young man. He wore wide pants and a loose fitting, beige tunic shirt made of hemp. His left arm was in a sleeve, and he had tied the other sleeve and half of his shirt into a sash at his waist. This left a muscular arm and part of his chest uncovered. His trousers flowed loosely to his knees; tight leggings covered his legs from his knees to his ankles. He wore sandals.

He faced fifteen other monks of all ages. Sweat glistened on his shaved head and left dark spots on his tunic. He stood slightly taller and broader than his pupils and carried himself with confidence.

The monk extended his left arm from his shoulder, pointing his palm up and outward and bending his thumb into his palm. He focused intently on his left fingertips. His right hand formed a fist near his ear. He balanced on his right foot and lifted his left leg high off the ground, pointing his toes toward the ground.

The others concentrated and repeated his movements.

The young teacher's brown, almond shaped eyes constantly scrutinized the group, noting their movements and any actions that appeared out of place.

A student lost his balance. The teacher thumped the boy on his head and told him what to do.

Jeffrey's eyes glazed over with excitement. "They're having class!"

"It's important that we stay together." Sabumnim rounded up Charlotte who was trying hard to attract the attention of one of the meditating monks. Sabumnim grabbed her waving hand and backed her away. When they looked up, Jeffrey had already gone outside.

Charlotte ran to the door and gazed in astonishment at the noisy courtyard thronging with people. "I can't see Jeffrey."

"This way. He's just on the other side of those teenagers." Sabumnim walked down the steps and Charlotte hurried after him.

They strode past boys arguing points of Buddhism while their teachers listened. Each youth wore his straight black hair combed back from his forehead and plaited into two braids which hung down his back.

Charlotte paused.

The oldest boy's brown eyes flashed spiritedly. "But according to the noble truths, existence is suffering."

An instructor monk with a long, stringy beard tapped the shoulder of the clean-shaven monk sitting next to him and nodded his head in agreement with the youth.

"But it goes beyond that." The younger boy scratched his ear and explained.

This time, the clean-shaven monk nodded in agreement and the bearded monk disagreed.

"We have to keep moving," Sabumnim said. "I'm losing sight of Jeffrey."

"I see him." Charlotte slipped ahead of Sabumnim and into the crowd. She called back over her shoulder, "He's by the wall doing kicks with the others."

Music blared forth from a group of boys practicing instruments. The sudden sound startled Charlotte, and she stopped. A boy blew low, haunting notes through a long trumpet, taller than he was. The other end of the trumpet balanced on the ground.

Young boys playing smaller instruments paraded around the courtyard. A shy boy shuffled along with his head lowered, not making eye contact with anyone, but following the heels of the boy in front of him. He held a small drum on a stick which he rotated whenever he remembered to do so. The beads hanging from the top of the drum clattered sharply against the drumhead.

Behind him, a pleasant faced boy looked right at Charlotte before squeezing his eyes shut and excitedly clashing the cymbals. His arms and head vibrated with the force of the clang and his two long braids jiggled on his back.

Sabumnim caught up to her. "Stay with me." He searched the crowd. "I don't see Jeffrey."

"Wait!" Charlotte pulled him over to a row of teenagers sitting cross-legged.

The first boy in line closed his anxious eyes and sat motionless. A wrinkled, pale-skinned monk, wielding a large, flat knife, leaned over the boy. Grabbing one of the boy's braids, the monk sliced through the thick plaits. Then wetting the teen's head, the monk shaved the boy. Clumps of black hair fell to the ground to be blown away by the wind. The monk grinned at Charlotte and pointed to her head with his knife. Charlotte reached protectively for her ponytail and backed into Sabumnim.

"Over there," he said.

Together, they darted through groups of younger boys sitting cross-legged and playing stick games. A mischievous boy yanked a braid of the rosy-cheeked child kneeling next to him. The child shouted and grabbed the instigator. They wrestled and rolled on the ground, blocking Charlotte's path. The others backed away and yelled encouragement.

A short, stocky monk planted himself over the fighters and seized each boy by a shoulder. He lifted them high in the air, before setting them down. His thin lips were pursed so tightly they disappeared into his round face. The other boys returned immediately to the game.

"Did you see that?" Charlotte looked around for Sabumnim.

He had gone ahead and stood by the wall, a forlorn expression on his face. The class was gone.

"Oh no, Sabumnim! Where did they go? Where's Jeffrey?" Charlotte anxiously wrung her hands.

"We're too late. Help me open the gate." He leaned his strong shoulder against the massive wooden door and pushed. Charlotte frantically added her small weight to the job. The slow moving door creaked open. They dashed through to the countryside.

Tears gathered in the corners of Charlotte's eyes. "How are we ever going to find him? There are so many roads."

Roads ran everywhere: to the snow-topped mountains, to the green valleys and to the sparkling sea. And yet, there was no sign of Jeffrey.

Charlotte's shoulders slumped dejectedly. Sabumnim laid a comforting hand on her head and scanned the horizon for any sign of movement.

"I'm not sure." He rubbed his chin. "There are so many possibilities. He could have gone with the young Buddhist monks to Koguryo. Or he could have touched the ribbon and gone ahead to find the Hwarangdo youth group. Or he could . . ."

"Jeffrey liked the monks!" Charlotte excitedly interrupted.

Sabumnim nodded.

"Koguryo," Charlotte said at the same time they touched the ribbon.

The mist rose.

# 4
## The Raid

Sabumnim and Charlotte landed with a thud on a hillside in the middle of flowering, pink camellia bushes. Hearing sounds of wailing in the distance, they scrambled out of the bushes. Branches tore at their clothes. Waxy, green leaves dropped from Sabumnim's hair.

They stood on an ancient footpath. The sorrowful singing came from a long line of grieving people trudging up the hill. Somber men led the procession, holding lanterns and waving a red funeral banner. Behind them, men carried a heavy, wooden bier holding a coffin.

The coffin was shaded by a broad piece of hemp cloth attached to the bier's frame. Three tassels made of red and white silken cords dangled from each corner of the shade. Diamond shaped red and white ornamental knots were knotted into each tassel.

A bell ringer followed the coffin and led the relatives, friends and villagers singing. Men wearing grotesque masks and waving burning sticks stalked back and forth along the outside of the parade of mourners.

Charlotte pulled at Sabumnim's jacket.

"They're scaring away evil spirits," he said.

The mourners were dressed similarly in funeral clothes. The rough, beige fabric was woven from the fiber of the hemp plant. The cloth covered each person's entire body. The men wore rice straw sandals and large cone-shaped hats woven of slender reeds. The wicker mourning hats covered three-quarters of the face and tied under the chin. Several women covered their dark hair with flat, square pieces of hemp while others tied white ribbons in their black hair.

Many of the mourners waved feathers in the air. Charlotte looked at Sabumnim. "They believe it helps the soul on its trip," he said.

Sabumnim searched for Jeffrey's reddish-blond hair in the crowd. He disgustedly folded his arms. "Ribbon?"

Charlotte slipped into the throng moving toward the stone tomb which nestled among others built into the peaceful, treeless hillside.

"Charlotte?" Sabumnim looked around.

People shuffled aside as a bouncing pony-tail moved through the procession. Sabumnim quickly found an opening and followed her.

The funeral procession stopped in front of the tomb. Charlotte was stuck in the crowd. She crouched and crawled close enough to see inside the tomb. Lacquered oil paintings of unicorns, blue dragons, and galloping horses decorated the walls, creating colorful murals. Detailed carvings showed men wrestling and others who appeared to be dancing.

Sabumnim found her.

"Some of their moves in the carvings look like our punches and blocks," Charlotte said.

"Because we're in Koguryo, it is probably *Subak*. It's one of the martial arts brought by the monks from China. *Taek Kyun,* Korea's own martial art, began in the south with the Hwarangdo."

Charlotte twisted her neck and searched the weeping crowd. "I don't see him." She pouted.

"I don't either."

They worked their way to the back of the mourners.

"I was sure Jeffrey would come this way," Charlotte said.

"Jeffrey?" A monk, the beginnings of a beard darkening his face, left the others. His badly sewn mourning clothes hung loosely on his body; the ragged edges covered his fingertips and toes. He stumbled, breaking a few stitches. The monk pushed his sleeves up, but they slid down again.

"Have you seen him?" Sabumnim's forehead wrinkled in concern.

"Jeffrey left with some of the monks for a village south of here." The monk scratched his wrist where the funeral cloth rubbed against his skin.

Charlotte's chin quivered. "We're never going to find Jeffrey."

"It's a place to start."

Sabumnim thanked the monk and started walking down the hillside. Charlotte fell in behind him, her head hanging. Near the bottom, they turned south on the twisting path.

"I have a game for you. Do you remember all those unfamiliar terms we used in class?"

"Yes." Charlotte listlessly kicked a pebble. It rolled toward a stream flowing next to the path. She sighed. "I don't know how many I remember."

"I will teach you how to remember them, and then you can teach your brother." Sabumnim moved his arms in tight circles. "Chug, chug, chug."

"That's a train," Charlotte mumbled. She followed indifferently behind him.

"Faster. Chug, chug, chug, chuggie, chuggie, chuggie. Kick your feet up, up, up. Let's get this train moving!"

Charlotte halted and stared in disbelief at Sabumnim kicking up dust and pumping his arms. A squirrel crossing the path dropped the walnut from its mouth, sat on its hind legs and scolded Sabumnim. Charlotte laughed, squinched her nose at the squirrel and began slowly moving her arms and feet, repeating Sabumnim's actions. She picked up speed.

"Chug, chug, chug, chuggie. I know what this is! It's an *ap chagi*, a front kick. Jeffrey's going to like this game! My turn. I want to do one."

Charlotte swung her back leg in a wide circle in front of her body until it was over her head. She pulled it sharply to the ground. "Now let me do this near you. Get it, Sabumnim? Near you!"

Sabumnim chuckled. "Got it. It's a *naeryu chagi*, an axe kick, right?"

"Right."

They heard sharp, hollow thumps and laughter. Six women knelt next to the slow moving stream. Their long, black hair was pulled back and tied in knots at the bases of their necks. The older women covered their hair with rough, hemp scarves.

The women soaked dirty clothes in the stream, spreading the wet fabrics on rocks, and pounding the white cloth with flat sticks. When each piece was clean, the women laid the laundry on large, flat rocks to bleach and dry in the sun.

One woman glanced briefly at Charlotte and Sabumnim and laughed. Dimples creased her cheeks. She mimicked Charlotte and swung her stick in a naeryu chagi motion, creating a new beat.

The other young women nodded their heads to the rhythm and took up the motion.

An older, squarely built woman listened and lightly tapped her stick. Her eyes lit up, and she chuckled. Sliding her sleeves up her arm, she pounded in the traditional up and down motion, a steady base to the rapid counter point of the circular thumps. Their laughter grew.

"How would you like to wash your clothes in the river?" Sabumnim said. "There's no running water or washing machines in this time."

"It looks like fun. I'll have to tell Mom and Dad about it." Charlotte skipped to the next tree. "Maybe we can wash our clothes that way, too."

A woman came up the path toward Sabumnim and Charlotte. Like the women washing clothes, she wore two pairs of trousers; the longer pair fell just short of her ankles and hung loose over her straw sandals. Her dark-brown hair coiled around her head and formed a base on which she balanced a large, gray earthenware pitcher. She removed the pitcher and held it in the stream, letting the water flow into it. Then she bent and lifted the pitcher onto her head.

Charlotte found a large piece of bark and set it on top of her ponytail. Her body wobbled from side to side as she tried to keep the bark balanced.

"Look at me!" Charlotte carefully turned on her toes to face the friendly woman.

The woman laughed and waved. Her hand faltered and dropped in horror to her mouth. Her laughter turned to shrieks, and she gestured wildly at the darkening sky.

Charlotte started. She whipped around, and the bark flew to the ground.

Not too far off, black smoke rose from the roofs of huts in their small Shillian hillside village.

"Jeffrey!" Charlotte shrieked.

The smoke from each individual fire joined together with the others to form a menacing column wide enough to block out the sun.

The women left their laundry and dashed screaming and wailing past Charlotte.

"Don't touch the ribbon!" Sabumnim warned. Fear deepened the lines on his face, and he raced desperately toward the fires.

Charlotte, running and skidding on the dirt path, tried to keep up. Soon she lost sight of Sabumnim and the women.

Charlotte finally reached the village. Wisps of smoke curled and twisted around her head, blocking her view. She coughed. Shouts, screams, and stampeding feet surrounded her, sounding weird and hollow within the treacherous smoke screen.

"Charlotte, hide!" A familiar voice yelled.

Charlotte fell to her knees and rolled quickly under bushes. Horses galloped by at full speed, their hooves throwing stinging clumps of dirt and dust at her. Holding her breath, Charlotte peeked through cupped fingers at the turmoil around her.

A soldier on horseback slowed. The cuffs of his short, padded jacket rode up his arm as he swiped an unlit torch from the warrior riding next to him. He dipped the torch into the red-gold flames of a burning roof and swung the fiery torch teasingly over the heads of a few trembling peasants.

A man backing out of a smoke filled house staggered into the side of the soldier's horse. The horse bucked. The soldier snarled and swiped the burning torch at the man.

The friendly woman dashed from the bushes and pulled her husband away from the horse's hooves.

Jarred out of their numbed state, the frightened villagers shrieked and stumbled toward the barley fields. Some separated from the main group and raced in the direction of the mountains.

Panicked animals tore in front of the soldiers and terrified villagers. A fat, squawking chicken jumped from a shed onto the head of a young teenager. With one arm, the boy shielded his eyes from the crazed hen's sharp claws. With his other, he grabbed the chicken by her tail feathers and yanked her off his hair.

The soldier flicked the flaming torch onto a thatched roof. He stood in his saddle and approvingly reviewed the destruction of the village. He bellowed a command and bolted to the fields a half-mile away.

The villagers who had taken refuge in the fields, screamed and lurched out of the soldier's way. He trampled the crop, causing as much damage as possible before finally entering the forested hills. His men raced after him.

The friendly woman's frightened children gathered around her, their brown eyes still showing terror. Her husband shakily stood.

The woman picked up her youngest child and paced nervously. She smoothed her daughter's single braid and shushed her quiet whimpering. The little girl sniffled and rubbed her short nose with a dirty hand.

Charlotte wiggled out from under the bush and shook the dust from her ponytail.

"Charlotte! Are you all right?" Sabumnim rushed from another burning house with an elderly man in his arms. He set the man safely away from the flames.

Once on the ground, the toothless man weakly straightened his high crowned hat with its broad brim on top of his gray topknot. Soon he was surrounded and fussed over by the women in his family.

"Sabumnim, why did they burn the houses? Are they coming back? I don't like it here." Charlotte stamped her foot, demanding an answer.

Excited voices echoed Charlotte's questions. The

villagers staggered back from the trampled fields and hills.

Some of the villagers watched the fires burn, while others ran toward the river with jars. Mothers held their sobbing children, and older men gathered helplessly in a close knot in the town square. Their lacquered horsehair hats bobbed erratically as they argued among themselves.

A farmer separated from the group and called out to a flushed, young man in his early teens. The teenager listened. He tightened the sash at his waist and straightened his shoulders. His single dark brown braid hung down the center of his back. The wind whipped his wide, white trousers around his thin legs. Barefoot, as were all the farmers, he trudged past the colorful Shamin devil-post standing guard on the outskirts of the village and followed the winding path up the mountainside.

"We can hide earlier next time. I sent Yeon Chul higher up the hill to keep watch." The farmer wiped his muddy hands on his smudged, loose fitting, short jacket.

"I know what I'd do if they burnt my house." Charlotte jumped into a fighting stance.

"We can do nothing." The friendly woman's husband hit his thighs in frustrated anger. "We are only farmers. They are trained soldiers with weapons and horses. This was only a warning to our king. Next time, it'll be worse. By the end of the season we'll probably have to pay taxes to a new king, and it doesn't matter whether he's from Baekje or Koguryo."

Charlotte recognized the defeat in the man's tone and her hands dropped uselessly to her side.

"Hey!" A well-known voice called.

Charlotte stared in amazement. Lugging river water in a wide-mouth, gray, clay jar, Jeffrey hurriedly passed the few others carrying water to the fires. Water sloshed over the edge and created tiny patches of mud in the road.

Jeffrey tossed the water on a burning roof. A bundle of thatch separated and tumbled onto the ribbon floating inches off the ground. A thin layer of mist rose from the ribbon and enveloped the thatch. When the mist evaporated, the thatch had disappeared.

"I've been looking for you, and do I have stories to tell!" Jeffrey said.

"Jeffrey!" Charlotte sprang toward him. "I knew it was your voice. I'm so glad to see you."

"Watch out for the ribbon!" Sabumnim lunged for her and caught her sleeve.

But it was too late. The mist rose.

# 5
# War

The sun's rays brightened the tips of the green fields swaying in the breeze.

"Now where are we?" Charlotte sat in water and mud between rows of short stalks.

Sabumnim had splashed down in the row ahead of her and sat facing her. He lifted his hands from the mud and softly wiped them on a plant.

Charlotte felt something slide gently over her foot. She looked down. A three-foot brown snake slithered over her toes, lifted its head and poked out its tongue. Charlotte squealed, jumped and kicked the snake toward Sabumnim. "I hate this ribbon! I hate being wet! Let's find Jeffrey and go home!"

Sabumnim calmly picked up the twisting snake and tossed it a few rows behind Charlotte. "It's okay, Charlotte. We're in a rice paddy. The ribbon says it's 630 A.D. We're in the same place only it's almost 100 years later."

"Then why is the village still burning?"

Shocked, Sabumnim spun around to see a section of

the village on fire and hundreds of armored soldiers approaching on horseback, about a half-mile away. They flourished long, deadly swords and spears. Flags and banners proclaimed they were warriors of the Baekje army.

Opposite them, a large Shillian army, poised for battle, sat on horses. The horses' armored bridles and chest braces would provide some protection in the battle to come.

The Shillian soldiers wore tall, rounded helmets with high centerpoints. Flaps of heavy material lined the bottom of the helmets and protected their necks. Short-sleeved, heavily padded jackets covered long-sleeved undergarments. Wide leather girdles belted around their waists shielded their ribs and stomachs, and smaller versions protected their wrists. Their tight fitting trousers were covered with loose flowing layers of heavy material and their feet were encased in thick, leather boots.

Sabumnim pushed Charlotte down behind the scanty rice stalks and into the mud.

"Sabumnim, there's a snake in here!" Charlotte jumped up.

"Better snakes than soldiers!" Sabumnim searched in vain for the ribbon.

The horses of the Baekje army thundered across the fields.

Charlotte squatted behind the rice stalks.

The Shillian horsemen didn't move, but a group of armored Shillian men and boys stepped forward. They wore tall, rounded helmets, heavily padded jackets, and thick boots. The new group pulled arrows from their quivers and strung their bows. They arced their bows and shot the arrows into the oncoming mass of Baekje soldiers.

The Shillian horsemen charged, passing the archers. With earsplitting bellows and clanks of swords, the Baekje and Shillian warriors clashed.

Two rows in front of Sabumnim and Charlotte, hunched a frightened farmer tightly clutching his reed hat to his chest. His topknot shook in fear. He wiped the back of his hand over the long, scraggy beard on his chin. His short, rumpled white jacket had twisted loose and drooped raggedly over his belt. He glanced furtively at his family to see if they were all there.

His four sons knelt next to him, clenching their teeth and knotting their fists in frustration and anger. The youngest boy, about twelve years old, deliberately loosened his fingers and braced them on the nearest mound of rice stalks. He dug his bare toes into the mud. His long, dark brown braid slid slowly from one side of his back to the other as he calculated the number in the Baekje army.

To Charlotte's right, the rest of the farmer's family squatted in the rice paddy and huddled together in terror. Their faces were pale and drawn beneath their normally tanned skin.

The farmer's plump wife supported her elderly father-in-law with her arm. Her hair had pulled loose from her bun and hung in lank sections over the shoulders of her white short jacket. The farmer's oldest daughter resembled the friendly woman of 100 years ago. She held a baby and kept the younger children quiet, making them stay low in the mud.

The deafening sounds of battle and angry shouts came closer. The foot soldiers put down their bows, lifted their broad swords and shields, and entered the fight.

The young Shillian general's horse was struck with an arrow and fell to the ground. The general rolled off it. Standing his entire five feet, five inches and fearless, he faced a bearded horseman of the Baekje army. Whirling around with a flying reverse turning kick aimed at the warrior's head, the young leader leapt seven feet off the ground and knocked the Baekje warrior off his horse.

The Shillian leader turned rapidly to his right and confronted a Baekje foot soldier. The Shillian's armor moved gracefully with his movements.

The Baekje soldier charged. Sunlight flashed off the sword he held above his head. The Shillian general delivered a side kick with incredible speed to the Baekje soldier's knee, tumbling him to the ground in the midst of the raging battle.

Like magic, the young man's sword flew from his own scabbard into his hand. While the battle raged around him, he faced and defeated one foe after another.

"He's part of the Hwarangdo, and he's using Taek Kyun to defend himself," Sabumnim said.

The youngest of the farmer's sons stood, inspired by the young man's bravery. Mud dripped from his loose fitting jacket and pants. He was about four feet eleven inches tall with muscular shoulders already strong from working in the fields. Determination shone from his dark eyes. "The monks taught us how to defend ourselves. This is the time to use it."

One by one, the brothers stood and advanced toward the battle.

An armored Baekje foot soldier saw them and snorted. "You fools," he shouted. "I'll teach you your place." The soldier charged.

"Wow!" Charlotte splashed to her feet. "The farmer's son just kicked that guy in the gut. Now he has a sword!"

Rebellious shouts and yells came from farmers attacking from the fields and hills. Overwhelmed by the well-led and well-trained Shillian forces and the committed villagers, the Baekje soldiers retreated.

A boisterous cheer rose from the crowd. Families came out of hiding. They formed a human chain from the village to the river and passed containers of water up to the fires. Some ripped sections of burning thatch off houses and flung them to the ground where others kicked dirt on them and smothered the fires.

"We'll work together to replace the roofs and rebuild the village," a farmer said.

After the fires were under control, the villagers gathered around the Shillian army and its young general, Rhee Woo-Hyun.

Charlotte studied him. He was shorter than Jeffrey and appeared to be about seventeen years old. A newly healed scar ran from under his leather girdled wrist and ended in a stub where his little finger used to be on his left hand. He and the other young warriors carried themselves with confidence and grace.

General Rhee removed his helmet and placed it under his left arm. Like many of the warriors and the farmer's sons, he wore his black hair parted down the center, hanging in a long braid down his back.

The villagers and army fell silent.

"We have won a glorious victory over the kingdom of Baekje," General Rhee said. "All over Shilla, people are uniting and fulfilling the dream of our king. With the help of our 'big brother' China, our four kingdoms will be one nation. We will finally be masters of our own country."

"Will he know Jeffrey?" Charlotte anxiously asked Sabumnim.

"If your brother came this way, he should. We can ask him."

The general finished his speech and moved regally through the noisy crowd. One by one they bowed, alternately blocking his passage and opening a path for him.

The farmer, whose family had helped fight the army, bent his knees slightly and rested his palms on his knees. He bowed. His wife knelt and laid her forehead on the ground.

Charlotte couldn't stand another minute of waiting for General Rhee to make his slow progression to where she and Sabumnim stood.

"General. General!" Charlotte sprinted over the bowing villagers and stopped abruptly in front of the general. She grabbed his sleeve. Her face was flushed from the recent excitement and smudged with dirt. "I'm trying to find my brother." Her voice trembled with worry.

General Rhee bent his head to look at her, the stern expression still on his face.

Charlotte gulped, let go of his sleeve, and backed up. Taking a deep breath, she spoke again. This time, her voice was a little firmer. "Please help me find Jeffrey. Have you seen him?"

Understanding flowed into his brown eyes. "You're Charlotte."

Sabumnim hurried forward, carefully avoiding stepping on the women and children whose hands and heads touched the ground. He stood by Charlotte.

Some of the harshness returned to the general's face, and he studied them, especially Sabumnim.

Sabumnim bowed, never dropping his guard.

"So you're the ones who are lost." General Rhee returned the bow. "Jeffrey told me all about you. We will wait until after the celebration starts, and I will take you to him."

Charlotte squeezed back tears and started to speak.

"Don't worry little one," General Rhee said. "We will find Jeffrey when the time is right."

She sighed in resignation.

In the village square, the farmer's oldest daughter hurried over and set out three mats for them to sit upon. Her younger sister knelt and placed a bowl of water before the general and visitors. They washed their hands and faces.

The farmers in the village's band brought out instruments which had escaped the fires and organized themselves at one end of the village square. A man balanced a zither made from a single piece of paulownia wood against his shoulder and plucked its twelve strings with his fingers. Another farmer held an hour-glass shaped drum in the middle like a barbell and tapped out a tune. Music soon filled the air.

The villagers milled around the open area, smiling and talking, pleased they had taken a stand. The music's rhythm touched them, and they swayed and twisted, creating their own dances. No two dances were alike but some of the movements were. Many danced, walking and turning on their heels. At times, they bent their knees and lifted themselves gracefully from this position.

Charlotte's ponytail flipped forward and backward and from side to side as she tried to see everything. She could feel the joy of the dancing villagers.

A little girl with a quick smile approached Charlotte and invited her to dance. Charlotte hopped to her feet. They playfully twisted their bodies in time to the music, tilting to the right and left, their arms spread wide above their heads.

A middle-aged man hoisted a drum over his left shoulder and with a wooden mallet struck the animal skin stretched over the drum's head. The drum was so loud everyone stopped dancing. He struck again and the men and women formed lines and circled around the square. They stomped the ground, leaned over and clapped their hands to the rhythm.

Charlotte rejoined Sabumnim and General Rhee. "This dance looks like they're working in the fields."

"It is like that," Sabumnim said. "The village band often plays while the farmers work and keep time to the music."

Several old men, their white beards moving in the breeze, watched. They talked and smoked long pipes.

The sun set in a burst of deep pinks and purples. Its final rays covered the crowd with a warm golden glow. Still the music flowed from the musicians.

The women left the square and served rice and *kimchee* to the army.

General Rhee set down his wooden bowl. An elderly woman quickly scooped the bowl off the mat and backed away.

"Jeffrey should have returned from his mission when we arrive," the general said. "It's time to go." He ordered his men to march ahead and leave a supply ox with him.

Charlotte waved good-bye to the little girl.

At the edge of town, the ribbon waited for them, a slight ripple marring its perfect peace. Charlotte and Sabumnim cautiously stepped over it.

General Rhee, who couldn't see the ribbon, watched their exaggerated movements. "You have some unusual customs in your land."

Sabumnim winked playfully at Charlotte. "Let's go get Jeffrey."

# 6

# The Hwarangdo

The morning sun's rays tentatively peeked through the forest of dark green dwarf pine, walnut and nut pine trees. Light fog drifted between the trunks, sometimes swallowing the travelers whole and the next moment freeing them from its tentacles.

The slow moving ox nudged Sabumnim in the back. Sabumnim stumbled.

Charlotte chuckled. "Good morning, Sabumnim."

"Easy for you to say. You've been riding!" Sabumnim grumbled. He stretched, and a few joints creaked loudly in protest.

"Good morning, Charlotte," the general said. He stopped, took a deep breath of the fresh morning air, and did a couple of deep knee bends. His helmet, which hung from the belted leather girdle around his waist, bounced gently.

General Rhee abruptly stopped exercising. He stood still and strained to hear. A bird chirped a morning song, and the general frowned.

Charlotte looked questioningly at Sabumnim.

Sabumnim listened to the sounds drifting on the cool morning breeze.

The general's expression lightened. "Everything's all right. We're almost there." He marched swiftly ahead of them, his posture that of a warrior, a leader.

"Almost where?"

"To the Hwarangdo training camp," Sabumnim said. "Can you hear that?"

Beneath the chatter of the early morning birds, Charlotte heard a low rumble and what sounded like human voices. She nodded excitedly.

"This way." They followed General Rhee along the rocky path which led them deeper into the forest and higher up the mountain.

The young general stopped on a rocky ledge overlooking a lush, green river valley. Patches of fog still floated through the valley, gradually burning off as the sun rose higher in the sky. On the opposite side of the valley, they saw rows of long, low wooden buildings covered with tile roofs. Positioned between the low buildings and a temple, were two three-tiered, stone pagodas.

Five guards, posted strategically at high points around the military camp, pointed deadly bows and arrows at the travelers. At General Rhee's signal, they lowered their weapons.

Charlotte slid off the ox and looked down. She spotted swimmers racing against the white-capped current in a swiftly moving, muddy river. Large, gray rocks punctuated the river in mid-stream and interrupted the river's rapid flow.

A broad-shouldered teenager climbed onto the largest rock. The rushing water crashed into the base of the rock, sprayed high over his head and plummeted in heavy droplets onto his bare chest and head. The water fell into the rock's deep fissures and drained back into the river to gather its forces and attack the boy again and again. The boy stood in a deep walking stance, adjusting his balance to stand firm against the water's strength.

The strong current slammed another boy into the rock. He pulled himself out of the cold water. A fresh cut, left by the rock, slashed across his bare chest. His long braid sloshed a stream of water down his back.

The teenagers grappled and tried to push each other off the rock while withstanding the water's relentless pounding.

In the yard next to a pagoda, soldiers wearing padded jackets, helmets, and leather girdles faced each other in two lines. The leader shouted a  command, and the warriors pulled their swords out. Some were faster than others.

"Do it again!" the leader ordered. "React quickly. Watch your opponent's eyes and shoulders. I want you to pull your blade out before they finish moving. The sword is an extension of your arm." He whipped out his sword so quickly that Charlotte didn't even see the movement. "Fight!"

The warriors bowed to their partners and rapidly drew their swords. They charged, attacking and blocking, striking their blades high and then low. Their bodies danced, moving out of the way and maneuvering for an opening to strike.

On the hillside opposite Charlotte and Sabumnim, two bands of archers stepped forward in military precision. One group practiced stances and drawing their bows. They aimed, but no arrows soared through the air.

"They're perfecting archery techniques," Sabumnim said.

The other group snapped their bows. Arrows split the cold morning air and landed with solid thuds in the tree growing from the mountainside below the visitors. One arrow flew wide and whizzed over Sabumnim's head. Charlotte and Sabumnim instinctively ducked.

"Too slow," General Rhee said sternly. "Expect the unexpected."

In another area, a squad hurled spears toward targets outlined in rocks on the forested hillside. The teacher inspected the spears, two of which lay flat on the ground. He mumbled under his breath. Raising his voice, he said, "Do it again! Further. Harder." Again and again the young soldiers practiced, aiming for distance and accuracy.

Some teenagers sat cross-legged on mats under a shade tree and ignored the physical activity surrounding them. A monk guided them through lessons written in Chinese characters.

A boy placed a ceramic teapot on a short legged table next to the teacher. He formally poured tea for the teacher, handed the cup to him and bowed.

Another young man yawned and caught himself. He sat up straight and traced Chinese characters with his brush.

A steep rock face rose behind the ledge on which Sabumnim and Charlotte stood. A muddy helmet, its centerpoint missing, toppled onto the ledge. Charlotte picked it up and curiously jabbed her finger through the hole in the top. Loose stones tumbled out of the wide bottom of a crevice three feet above her head.

Filthy fingers grasped the opening, and a young boy jumped squarely onto the ledge in front of her. Startled, Charlotte yelped and dropped the helmet. Her eyes flew wide open and the blood drained from her cheeks.

"For crying out loud, Charlotte, it's only me," Jeffrey said. He wore the same thick uniform as the general. It was stained with sweat and soil. Charlotte didn't care. She excitedly wrapped her arms around him.

Sabumnim picked up the helmet, a rueful expression on his face. He handed it to Jeffrey over Charlotte's head. "I'm glad your armor held up."

"Me too, Sir!" Jeffrey saw Sabumnim's expression and quickly added, "It's not quite what you think, Sir."

"I hope not. We're supposed to be observing." Sabumnim raised his eyebrows.

"Jeffrey." Charlotte released him from her bear hug. "You've gotten some muscles."

"We've been training hard." He flexed his muscles, then he paused and grinned sheepishly. "Some of it's the thick armor we wear."

Hesitantly he held out his belt. "But look at my white belt. It's dirty and gray."

"It's okay. We can wash it for you. Right, Sabumnim?"

"No. You must never wash it. In the past, belts became black from years of wear. Today, belts are symbols of training. And when people look at your belt, they understand your accomplishment."

Charlotte held the ends of her white belt up to the sunlight. "Mine's just a little dirty."

"That's all right," Sabumnim said. "Learning martial arts is an individual journey that can last your whole life."

More stones clattered out of the hole in the mountainside, followed quickly by boys leaping onto the ledge. Like Jeffrey, they were tired and their armor was torn and streaked with mud.

Seeing their general in this unexpected location, they snapped to attention and bowed. A young man, glancing curiously at Sabumnim and Charlotte out of the corner of his eye, absentmindedly dragged the toe of his thick boot in the dirt.

General Rhee glared severely at the young man. "Did you retreat?" His voice sharply rasped the question. He frowned and his eyes formed mere slits as he waited impatiently for the answer.

"No, Sir!" The young man pulled himself straight and stopped dragging his foot. "It's an honor to serve, Sir. We were outnumbered, but we stood our ground. The villagers joined us when they saw we weren't giving up and we were winning."

"It is not in our code to retreat, Sir." A young man pole-vaulted on a six-foot branch out of the crevice. When he hit the ledge, he sagged briefly with exhaustion. His bloody thigh was bound with a strip of fabric. His face was pale but he stood tall in front of General Rhee.

Some of the severity left the general's face. "Go down to camp, clean up and eat. Report to me later." He briefly detained the last person to arrive. "Welcome back, little brother. You performed bravely?"

"Yes, Sir." A smile of satisfaction crossed both their faces. They bowed.

"I'll see you soon," Jeffrey whispered to Charlotte. He and the young soldiers formed two lines and marched down the winding path leading to camp. General Rhee's brother used the branch as a crutch and limped a short distance behind the others.

They passed a group of young men setting out on a mission. They weren't wearing padded armor, but white jackets of ramie and silk. Their wide bottomed trousers were bound tightly around their waists. Their hair was neatly combed and braided.

"It's time for our pilgrimage to the spirit of the mountain," a boy said to Jeffrey. "Have you been there yet?"

Jeffrey shook his head and, with his team, entered one of the wooden buildings.

"What's a code, General?" Charlotte squeezed her flat biceps muscle. They walked down the path to the camp.

"It's the set of rules we live by. It's based on Confucian and Buddhist principles." The general focused on an imaginary distant point, and he talked automatically, almost as if they weren't there. "The first rule is to be loyal to our king. The second is always to obey our parents."

"Always?" Charlotte sighed.

General Rhee chuckled and continued less intensely. "Yes. It's the respectful thing to do. The third is always be honorable to your friends. Number four, never retreat in battle. Number five, never kill just for the sake of killing."

The three passed the wet swimmers marching into camp. The swimmers' wide bottomed, white trousers clung in patches to their wet skin. They held themselves erect, trying to ignore the brisk wind sending shivers through their bodies.

"Brr! It's too early to go swimming," Charlotte said.

"We train in all kinds of weather; in the winter's cold and snow and in the summer's heat. It helps us to concentrate on what we need to do and not on how we feel at that moment. We train our minds as well as our bodies."

Jeffrey approached, balancing four glazed earthenware bowls of rice and four sets of bronze chopsticks. Another boy carrying mats and tea arranged a spot for the travelers under a spreading walnut tree.

"I hope you're hungry." Jeffrey bowed to the general and handed him his bowl. Then Jeffrey handed chopsticks and bowls to Sabumnim and Charlotte.

Charlotte stared helplessly at the rice.

"Here. Let me show you." Sabumnim handled the chop sticks with the familiarity of an old friend. "The bottom stick rests at the base of your thumb and is braced by your third and fourth fingers."

"Like I hold my pencil?"

"Right. The other stick is pinched between the thumb and forefinger and can move." Sabumnim demonstrated with his set.

Charlotte opened and closed her sticks. After a few unsuccessful attempts, her stomach growled. General Rhee handed Charlotte a bronze spoon. It looked like a miniature shovel, its oval shaped bowl almost flat.

"Chopsticks don't always work because of how we steam our rice," he said kindly. "Most of the time, we use spoons."

Charlotte smiled her thanks and hurriedly scooped up her rice. The spoon scraped the bottom of her bowl. Boys around them stopped and stared before returning to their own food.

"Charlotte," Jeffrey muttered, "that's bad manners."

"But I was hungry!"

Sabumnim finished his rice and put down his bowl. "Now that we've found you, Jeffrey, it's time for us to go." Sabumnim rose and brushed off his pants.

Jeffrey looked at General Rhee for permission to leave. "May I leave, Sir?"

The general nodded his head slightly. "Go with your Sabum. You have done your part for the Hwarangdo, but this is our battle." He paused and thought for a minute. Watching Sabumnim carefully, the young general added slyly, "You are but an observer."

"Unfortunately, that's not always proving to be the case," Sabumnim wryly pointed out. He bowed to General Rhee.

Jeffrey rose and bowed. He was torn with emotion: happy to be with his sister again and sad to leave his new friends. Charlotte excitedly rose and stood next to him and smiled broadly at the young general.

Returning the smile, General Rhee bowed.

# 7

# The Golden Age of Shilla

Sabumnim and the children hiked along the trail away from camp. Just before the trail divided, the ribbon settled restlessly over the path and blocked their passage. Popcorn puffs of mist danced around their ankles, and they carefully backed away.

"Now what do we do?" Charlotte asked. "It's not going to let us cross."

"I'm sure it will when it's ready." Sabumnim dodged a particularly large puff. "Watch."

The ribbon floated aside and peacefully allowed them to pass onto one of the paths.

The new trail led down the mountainside past fields of rice and a village to a large city surrounded by a high granite wall. They could see many gray L-shaped estates built around interior courtyards. The palace's green tiled roofs perched one upon another and rose above most of the other buildings. Some of the Buddhist pagodas rose seven stories high and towered above the palace. Woven into the ribbon's fabric was the year 680 A.D.

"It looks like a giant mall!" Jeffrey said.

"It's *Kyongju*, the walled capital of Shilla, where the royal family lives. A million people live here and work for the king."

"We've never been to a city before. Can we go down and take a look?" Jeffrey rocked restlessly back and forth on his feet.

"Charlotte?" Sabumnim waited patiently while Charlotte tightened her ponytail and straightened her belt. She chewed on her lower lip.

Finally Charlotte spoke. "I did want to go home, but I'd like to see the city first."

Without waiting for them, she skipped down the path. The plume of her ponytail skimmed the needles of the low hanging pine branches.

Caught unaware by her swift movement, Sabumnim and Jeffrey chuckled at each other, then quickly ducked under the branches and tried to catch up.

The dirt path gradually widened into a well- traveled road. The mountainous, pine covered ridges gave way to rolling fields of rice. Barefoot men and children bent over the rows of mounded earth and planted rice.

Ahead of the travelers trudged an old farmer, wearing a wide-brimmed, high crowned, lacquered horsehair hat over his topknot. The hat tied under his chin. On his back was an A-shaped frame which carried a load of sticks, and he leaned on a tall, crooked walking stick for support.

"Why is he carrying sticks on his back?" Charlotte asked.

"It's firewood to sell in the city. They don't have stores yet like the ones we use," Sabumnim said.

Walking up the road from the city was a younger man wearing a narrow hat over his topknot. The hat looked like an upside down flowerpot.

When the two men met in the roadway, they stopped, spoke to each other briefly, bowed, spoke and bowed again. Each man waited for the other to move forward.

"Why don't they just go on their way?" Jeffrey asked.

"Politeness is a very important custom. To pass each other right away would be rude," Sabumnim said.

At last, the older man walked past the younger man.

The younger man with the narrow hat proceeded on the path toward the three travelers. Reaching them, he paused, bowed, and told them to pass first.

"Thank you. But you go first." Sabumnim bowed.

The man bowed and continued.

"Why is his hat so different from the other man's and the ones we've seen before?" Charlotte asked.

"We're seeing a change in styles from the wide brimmed hats to narrow ones. Tradition has it that long, long ago a king was concerned about the amount of fighting among his people. So he had a new wide-brim hat designed. The king thought his people wouldn't fight if they were worried about damaging their hats."

"Didn't work, did it?" Jeffrey grimaced.

"Every country has a history of fighting. We are entering a time of peace and the styles are changing."

They passed the village and saw a group of rural

women gathered in the center square. Barefoot children played in the dirt near the community well. Several women talked and laughed while they waited their turn. One woman filled her tall, glazed earthenware jar with water. She bent her knees and lifted the jar to her head. A small boy and girl whined that the woman was leaving too soon. At her sharp command, they quieted and walked with her.

At a crossroads, they came upon a plump, older monk. His hair was growing back and cradled his round head with gray, stubby fuzz. Thick, black eyebrows streaked with gray highlighted his intelligent dark eyes.

The monk wore two robes. A white, v-necked robe reached his ankles and a blue overcoat flowed gracefully over the robe. A sword and a dented brass bowl hung from his sash.

Seeing them approach, the man untied his sword and laid it beside him. He lifted the twelve-string lute he carried on his back and sat cross-legged next to the path. "Come and sit for awhile." He plucked the strings with calloused fingertips.

"Wow." Jeffrey leaned forward for a better look at the polished wooden instrument. It was about three-feet long. "Where did you get that?"

"I made it. The rounded part of the box symbolizes heaven, the flat bottom represents earth and the twelve strings represent the months in a year. Try it."

Jeffrey plucked a simple modern melody from the strings.

"Hmmm. That's a new sound. Quite different." The monk took back his lute. "I'm Won Hyo. Let me play for you. I've found that everyone loves music."

He began chanting, his deep voice holding one note for a long time and then following the note with a rapid melody.

Fascinated, Charlotte, Jeffrey and Sabumnim sat cross-legged on the ground around Won Hyo.

"Do they give you money for playing?" Jeffrey asked. "Like the people I've seen in the park playing instruments and acting?"

"Money?"

Jeffrey handed him a quarter. "You know, like this. It's made of metal or paper and you can buy things with it."

"Oh." Won Hyo set the lute aside and fingered the quarter. "No. People trade for what they want." He sniffed it before handing it back to Jeffrey.

"What do you do?" Jeffrey put away the quarter.

"I meet people such as farmers and commoners on the road and in the wine shops. We sing songs. The royalty didn't like me much for talking with these people. They thought I was common, too. But they soon found I was the only one who could interpret Buddhist literature so they could understand it. Eventually I was accepted and even tricked into marrying a princess. My son, Sol Chong, has become a well-known scholar."

"I didn't think monks could marry," Jeffrey said.

"Some sects can. I wasn't supposed to, but I do what I want or what I'm tricked into." He set the lute in his lap and rubbed his fingers against the polished grain.

"Why do farmers and commoners listen to you?" Charlotte asked.

"I teach through song that they can reach salvation by praying rather than by studying Buddhist literature which is written in Chinese. Only royalty and the upper class have time to learn Chinese." He rubbed his hand over his fuzzy head. "Buddhism shouldn't be just for royalty."

"I bet you've travelled all over with your teaching. Have you been to China?" Jeffrey asked.

"I tried." Won Hyo's mouth twisted in a wry grin. "Twice. One time, I was almost arrested in Koguryo and tried as a spy. The other time, I reached enlightenment during my trip. So I quit trying to go to China to study." His eyebrows creased in a thoughtful frown. "I think I'm the only monk of my time not to make the trip."

He fell silent, but his restless fingers plucked another melody from the strings. Two men leaving the city, stopped to listen. Farmers wandered over from nearby fields. Three women balancing clay pots on their heads, paused. More and more people came to see what had attracted the others and gathered around the foursome.

Won Hyo began to sing and talk. Some men and women nodded in agreement. Others shook their heads, muttered to their friends and left.

Sabumnim tapped Jeffrey and Charlotte on their shoulders and motioned them to come with him. They backed silently through the crowd and finished their trek to the city.

The arched, stone gateway rose majestically over their heads as they entered the walled city. Single storied, mud-walled, gray tiled houses were built into the high walls surrounding the city.

Men and women busily walked to and from homes and workshops along the wide main street. A barefoot, middle-aged farmer in a short, girdled jacket trudged past them. Slung over his shoulder was a net bag woven out of straw. It bulged with potatoes. A woman carried a baby on her back in a wide sling tied around her waist. The baby fussed and chewed on his knuckles.

Four men carrying a large enclosed box on poles trotted around a corner onto the main road. The box's sides and top were made of dark fabric. Graceful fingers pushed the window drape aside. Charlotte was surprised to see the woman inside the box wore lipstick and eye make-up. Her pastel blue, silk blouse tied in a bow in front. Her skirt was a brilliant rose silk.

"What kind of box is that? Could I get a ride?" Charlotte's eyes lit up in anticipation.

"It's a palanquin," Sabumnim said. "Only the royal family use them for transportation."

"Oh." Charlotte pouted.

A barefoot woman wearing a short jacket and a short skirt over wide trousers picked up a dipper hanging by the city well. The dipper was made from half of a dried gourd shell from which the insides had been scooped out. She poured water into her stoneware container. The woman hung the dipper back up, balanced the container on her head and walked off in the direction of the palace.

"I guess she's not royalty," Charlotte said. "She has to walk too."

High above her head, Sabumnim's lips twitched.

Charlotte watched the men carry the palanquin to the tall, multiroofed palace. Animals created out of clay perched along the palace's roof ridges.

"Why is that building the only one to have animals on it?" she asked.

"It's the palace. Animals on the palace roof are meant to ward off evil spirits."

"Let's go down this street." Jeffrey pointed to the one from which the rich woman had ridden. "It's really busy." He turned left onto a narrow, winding, hard-packed dirt road.

Not far ahead of him, Jeffrey saw a Buddhist temple with a green tiled roof. He stepped off the main street. A narrow dirt path took him from the bustling city into another world. He wandered between red and yellow flowering bushes and circled a peaceful lotus pond. A frog croaked and splashed into the shallow pond, creating ripples on the smooth surface.

The temple's red, wooden door opened and a grating squeal destroyed the serene atmosphere. Five monks found their shoes on the top granite step and slid them on. The monks solemnly formed a straight line and walked down the steps and toward the palace.

The monastery door remained open. As soon as the monks were out of sight, Jeffrey sprinted up the steps and looked inside.

"Hey! Look at this," he yelled over his shoulder. "There's monsters in here!" He disappeared inside.

Charlotte dashed up the steps and stopped just outside the door. She peered hesitantly into the building's colorful interior. Jeffrey's hand clasped her wrist, and she muffled a scream. He pulled her inside.

"Look at those roof beams up there," he said. "They've got green and yellow monster faces painted on them."

Sabumnim strolled inside. "Monster tiles in the roof beams of Buddhist temples are a left-over from early Shamin beliefs. They scare away evil spirits. Religions often adopt traditions of a religion that's already accepted in an area. It's easier to get people to accept new beliefs that way." He marshalled them outside the temple.

They ambled down a side street's curving dirt path, gazing curiously at the tiled shops and workrooms crowded around them.

Jeffrey followed the path around a two room workshop.

"This shop has been plunked right in the middle of the street."

A short, round man carrying a large vase bustled out the front door and bumped into Jeffrey's back. Jeffrey shot forward, almost falling to his knees.

"Oh my. Oh dear. Oh my." The man spoke rapidly in a high, thin voice. He turned the tall vase over and over, checking the smoothness of the bottom edge and the upper rim.

"That's okay. I'm not hurt."

The man jumped. He squinted at Jeffrey and finally focused on him. "Oh my. I'm sorry. I didn't see you." He bowed rapidly. "The king is waiting to see my work. I must go."

"For the king! May I see it?" Jeffrey's eyes gleamed brightly.

Nervously tapping his straw sandaled feet, the man held out the stoneware vase. Traces of green and yellow glazes frosted one side.

"It's the latest from my kiln. For some reason the ash causes these colors to form on my pieces. It's always on the side away from the fire." The man frowned.

"Did you carve this dragon into it?"

"I etch all my work." He appeared to have forgotten his hurry and turned the piece over for Jeffrey to inspect.

"I think the king will like it. That's a cool dragon."

"The king! Oh my. I must go!" The man darted glances to his right and left. He clasped the vase into the crook of his arm. The flowing sleeve from his white, hemp jacket fell over the piece. He bowed once more to

Jeffrey, tightened his protective grip and rushed off.

Charlotte stepped onto the hard dirt floor of the makeshift shop. It was cool and dark and smelled of moist clay. Another craftsman held a red, round-bottomed bowl, etched with honeysuckle vines, up to the light from the door. He turned it this way and that. When Charlotte entered, he set the ten-inch high bowl down.

He nodded to her. Smudges of gray clay slashed artistically across the front of his jacket and pants. He rolled up his sleeves and his pants' legs and sat down at a kickwheel. He slapped a clump of dark, grayish black clay in the center and pumped his feet to turn the wheel round and round.

Charlotte edged closer. "Where do you buy the clay?"

"Buy? We don't buy it. This dirt is all around our city. It belongs to the king. This bowl will be for the king, too."

Using his hands and the motion of the wheel, the potter formed a wide-mouthed bowl. "We try to supply

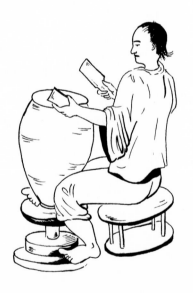

many of the king's needs for beautiful objects. Sometimes, though, we trade for goods. See that dagger edged with colorful enamel work?"

Charlotte wandered closer to the shelves.

"I got it off of a trader from Central Asia just yesterday."

"It is pretty."

The man absentmindedly nodded. His hands expertly shaped the clay.

"But I really like this one." Charlotte stood on tiptoe and pointed toward a foot-high, gray, unglazed stand which held three curved horns.

She grazed one of the horns with her little finger. The horn wobbled in its thin bracket. She gasped, a quick intake of breath. She pulled her hand back. Careful not to make a sound, she slowly looked over her shoulder at the man. He was engrossed in his work. Holding her hands behind her back, Charlotte quietly left.

Jeffrey entered a nearby coffin shop. Many of the small, stoneware coffin jars were etched with flowers; lotus blossoms were the most common.

"The monks believed in cremation." Sabumnim tapped Jeffrey's shoulder. "Let's go. I'd like to see the different styles of tiles."

"Think they'll have tiles with monster faces on them?" Jeffrey asked hopefully.

Sabumnim shrugged. "You can look."

They entered a workshop containing many unusual roof tiles and sculptures. A Buddhist monk searched through stacks of tiles. The bottom of his robe snagged on a two-foot high sculpture of a horse dressed for battle. The monk gingerly gathered his robe tightly around his body and held it with one hand. His other hand rapidly separated tiles. He glanced at a few fancy tiles etched with faces and flowers, but lingered over green glazed, rounded tiles. He tapped them.

"The king has ordered these for the new temple."

Charlotte entered a jewelry workshop. The jeweler glanced briefly at her, then turned back to the gentleman from the palace. The craftsman selected a heavy gold necklace and looped it over his arm.

"This is one of my favorites. Notice the rich, green jade inlaid in the thick gold rope. And you can see your reflection in the black stones. What do you think?" He held up matching, dangling gold earrings.

The visitor laid long, narrow fingers over his mouth, balancing his pointed chin in the palm of his hand. He wore two jackets: a pastel blue silk jacket covered by a long silk overcoat. His wide trousers were gathered at the waist, and he wore black slippers.

At last he shook his head. "Not for me. I want something more elaborate."

Charlotte's mouth dropped. Snapping her jaw shut, she left and found Sabumnim.

"There are so many beautiful things. I didn't know they could do all this so long ago."

"People now have the time to be creative," Sabumnim said. "Because of the Hwarangdo's help in uniting the country, everyone is living a richer life. We're in the Golden Age of Shilla."

"I'm glad we came." Charlotte took one last look around at the bustling crowds of farmers, tradesmen, and palace servants.

"Me too," Jeffrey said.

The ribbon stretched before them. It led through a side gate of the city and past a few mud-walled homes located outside the safety of the city's high walls. Sabumnim and the children followed. The warm sun beat down upon them.

"Where else can the ribbon take us? What about a seaport?" Jeffrey flicked an imaginary fishing rod.

"The harbor of *Pusan* should do." Sabumnim reached for the ribbon.

# 8

# Pusan Harbor

When the mist cleared, Sabumnim and Charlotte knelt on two tall stacks of tightly bound bales of hemp. The hemp's rough stalks scratched Charlotte's knees. She jumped off and landed on one of the many stepping stone paths crisscrossing the wharf's hard-packed earth. Sabumnim landed beside her and brushed stray hemp straws off his pants.

"Phew!" Charlotte crinkled her nose. "It smells like dead fish."

Sea gulls shrieked and dove toward fish guts floating on the murky, brown water.

Several fishermen sat on the ground next to the day's catch. Their short, loose, white jackets were wet and dirty. They had rolled up their sleeves and strapped their wide trousers from their knees to their ankles so the pants wouldn't flap loose. They were barefoot.

The fishermen slit the bellies of the fish, pulled out the insides and threw them into the water where the gulls fought over the remains. The fishermen then tossed the gutted fish into a large, wooden vat.

"Help!" Jeffrey sprawled on top of a huge stack of baled hemp carried by four muscular dock workers. The bales balanced uneasily across two long poles and wobbled under Jeffrey's weight. With a look of desperation, Jeffrey clung by his fingertips to the edges of the top bale for support. His legs bounced from side to side.

A worker slapped Jeffrey's foot. "Don't move!"

"Hey!" Jeffrey jerked his foot out of the worker's way.

The bales tilted. The workers frantically adjusted their gait to keep their load balanced. But it was no use. The bales quivered and toppled toward the deep vat of gutted fish.

Wide-eyed and helpless, Jeffrey rode the bales down into the day's catch.

"Get out of our fish, you little thief!" Fishermen jumped up from cleaning fish and bolted toward the vat.

Jeffrey panicked and tried to push his way out from beneath the prickly bales of hemp and slimy fish. He gasped for air. But the fish, piled up to his waist, were wet and slimy. Jeffrey's feet slipped. He slid backwards, his arms flailing as he sank beneath the fish again.

The angry dock workers tried to rescue their bales before the fish oil destroyed them. They pushed the fishermen back. A fight broke out.

"Uh oh," Charlotte said. "Jeffrey's done it again."

Dodging the battling fishermen and dock workers, Sabumnim reached the vat. Jeffrey finally found footing on a sinking bale. Sabumnim grabbed and pulled, but lost his grip on Jeffrey's slimy wrist. Jeffrey's arms thrashed, and he slipped under again.

Sabumnim ducked a flying punch. Bracing his feet on the outside of the vat, he found Jeffrey's sleeves and twisted them tightly around Jeffrey's wrists. Sabumnim yanked. Jeffrey popped from the vat onto the wharf and knocked Sabumnim backwards.

Jeffrey slid over Sabumnim's head, skimming on his stomach head first into the water. Disturbed during feeding, the steel-gray and white gulls shrieked and flew upwards.

Jeffrey splashed out of the dirty water. A dock worker stuck his angry, weathered face in front of Jeffrey who nimbly sidestepped the furious man and darted toward Charlotte hiding in the shadow of hemp bales waiting to be loaded onto the next ship.

The battle boiled around Sabumnim and the vat. Sabumnim blocked, ducked and pushed his way out of the fight. He located Charlotte and Jeffrey, and they sprinted toward an alley, leaving the enraged fighters behind them.

Soon the three were lost in the port's endless maze of warehouses and narrow alleys.

"I'm glad we're out of there!" Jeffrey stopped and bent over with his hands on his knees. He struggled to take deep breaths.

"Are you ever soaked." Charlotte's breath came in shallow gasps. She stared and pointed. "Jeffrey!"

"Huh?" Jeffrey stared uncertainly at his jacket. It popped out at odd intervals, first at his stomach, then by his side, and back to his stomach again.

Charlotte laughed. "What's happening to your shirt?"

"I don't know, but it tickles." Jeffrey felt inside his jacket and chased something around. Finally, he pulled out a small fish and tossed it aside. "And stinks!"

"Look at all the stuff." Charlotte gazed at their new surroundings.

The narrow path curved up and down an area of sloping ground and swung around unevenly spaced, wooden warehouses. The three travelers separated and wandered among the buildings and goods being prepared for shipping.

Empty wooden crates were piled haphazardly next to a building at the top of the hill. Chinese characters painted in red brightened up a wall and a latticed window shutter.

Charlotte wanted a closer look at the characters. She pushed several wooden crates together, lifted one on top of the others and climbed up. Her head was even with the window. She touched the wooden characters, her head resting against the lattice shutter covering the window.

A scowling face appeared and glowered at her.

Surprised, Charlotte jumped off the crates. She ran around the corner and bumped into a tall, yellow roll of silk tilted upright against the wall. It wobbled. She steadied the roll. Dozens of other colorful, circular bolts perched next to it. Loose fabric edges draped carelessly in front of each roll. A piece of the bright yellow silk slid gracefully over her wrist.

Charlotte was entranced. She twined the colorful ends around her short fingers, mixing and matching the colors until she found a combination of blue, red, and yellow she liked.

"What are you doing?" The Chinese warehouse owner rushed around the corner. He stood threateningly on the slope in front of her. His long, silk overcoat twisted around his legs.

"Oh!" Charlotte jerked her hand away and squeezed in the tiny space between the building and silks.

"Come out!" He grabbed at her.

She jumped away. Her quick movement popped a red bolt away from the wall. It teetered for a breathtaking second and fell forward on the warehouse owner. He shoved it back, jarring the remaining bolts away from the wall.

Charlotte watched. Everything seemed to move in slow motion.

A few bolts slid sideways and fell to the ground. Others bounced off the owner and tumbled down the slope, unraveling yards of colorful silks. The owner frantically fled after the bolts. He grabbed the flying ends and yanked backwards, unwinding the fabric even faster.

"No!" He dropped the fabric and raced after the rolling bolts. He tripped over a shiny, rose colored silk bolt. Several bolts bounced over him. He tumbled down the hill; the rainbow colored silks tangled around his body. Bumping against a wall, he came to an abrupt, stop. The man grunted hoarsely as the final bolts thumped against him.

Sabumnim found Charlotte. She was speechless.

"Let's move inland," he said. "We seem to be destroying the wharf."

They scrambled away from the warehouse and

dashed down the alley. The ribbon appeared momentarily, directing them to a smaller footpath, then vanished.

The warehouses grew further and further between and finally disappeared. The dirt path gradually widened and rolling rice paddies appeared. Farmers bent over the rice, harvesting the crop. A young woman stretched and rubbed her lower back. A child pulled at her skirts. She shook her head, and both child and mother bent over the rice.

In the distance, a small village nestled at the base of a pine covered mountain. Coming toward them, trudged an ox carrying pine brush strapped to a rig on his broad back and an old farmer who peered at the travelers through ancient, brown eyes. He wore no hat over his gray topknot and leaned on a tall, thick bamboo stick. Every so often he'd slap the ox with the bamboo, guiding the ox along the path.

The man stopped and waited for Sabumnim and the children to pass. Sabumnim halted and asked him to continue first.

"Some of the customs continue for a long time." Jeffrey watched the man and his ox plod relentlessly along the road.

Still following the path, the travelers left the fields behind them. The sun sank lower in the deepening blue sky, setting the bottom of the clouds aflame. The walls of a city were silhouetted in deep shadow against the flaming sky.

The travelers entered the city and arrived at a courtyard of a richly decorated Buddhist temple. Stone paths curved between quiet, green gardens. The temple stood seven stories high. Two flights of granite steps led to the first floor of the temple. Each of its seven green-tiled roofs, one narrower than the one spaced a floor below it, angled downward and then tilted up at the outer edge.

"Looks like small brick ski jumps, the way they curve up at the ends," Jeffrey said.

"The tile roofs are curved for the same reason the roads are crooked," Sabumnim said. "Notice the Buddhist figures on each level? They all have their part in repelling evil spirits."

"What kind of flowers are those?" Charlotte pointed upwards.

"Lotus blossoms," Sabumnim said. "And, those . . ."

"Animals are dragons." Charlotte triumphantly finished his statement.

"I wonder if they have monster masks on their roof beams, too?" Jeffrey said.

"I'm sure you'll find the tiles are there," Sabumnim said.

On the ground floor, two stone lions guarded a wide door on each side of the pagoda. Young men, deep in conversation, walked down the pagoda's steps and passed a monk ceremoniously lighting granite lanterns alongside the curving paths. Other people moved in and out of the pagoda or sat on the stone benches.

Charlotte skipped closer to the nearest gray lantern. Two stone lions standing on their back legs balanced the lantern between them, using their noses and front paws. She tentatively rubbed the lion's cold mane.

Several monks left the temple, walking in a straight line down the steps. Wooden dinner bowls bounced gently against the sides of the monks' robes.

Jeffrey wandered along the path and stopped near enormous, stone feet, each with six toes, shaded by flowering bushes. His head tilted backwards. A statue of Buddha towered twenty feet above him, gleaming red in the setting sun. Charlotte and Sabumnim joined Jeffrey.

The young men walked behind the travelers, their silken trousers and jackets rustling softly. Slender hats covered their topknots. "Pak Seung-Hee is working at the observatory," one of the young men said to his friends. "He's tracking a new star. He thinks it may have some effect on the security of the royal family. Let's go see if he'll let us look at it."

Jeffrey's eyes lit up with excitement. Sabumnim and Charlotte grinned at Jeffrey, and they set off after the young men.

# 9
# The Observatory

Gathering clouds covered the moon leaving patches of scattered starlight to brighten the path up the hillside. The observatory, a sixteen-foot wide tower of stone bricks, loomed almost thirty feet above them.

"It looks like one of those old-fashioned milk bottles that used to be delivered door to door," Sabumnim said.

Jeffrey's and Charlotte's blank faces stared at Sabumnim.

"Never mind," Sabumnim shook his head.

The dome opened to the sky. At the top, a lone, shadowy figure stood by instruments which had been built to study the moon and stars. He waved to the young men.

"Seung-Hee! We want to see the stars before it rains," the young men yelled before entering the dark doorway. Half-way up the tower, the light from their lantern flashed out a window, brightening the countryside.

"Put out the light. It ruins my vision," Seung-Hee said.

Darkness overtook the travelers.

Jeffrey walked around the tower. "I thought astronomy wasn't studied until the 1400s. We're in the 600s and here's an observatory!"

"Ancient people believed the moon and stars guided their futures, and by studying the stars they could predict storms, earthquakes, or wars. Most importantly, they charted stars and comets and developed calendars."

"Look, Sabumnim, between those dark clouds. It's the Big Dipper!" Jeffrey said.

Sabumnim stood next to Jeffrey, and they stared at the stars.

"And there's the North Star," Sabumnim said. "Sailors all over the world used it for centuries to guide them across the oceans."

The wind picked up and clouds glided faster across the stars, creating a patchwork of light and dark.

"Who else is down there?" Pak Seung-Hee leaned over the edge.

"We're travelers looking at the stars," Sabumnim said.

"Travelers?" Seung-Hee's voice raised with excitement. "Where have you been?"

"We've been to Koguryo and China," Jeffrey said.

"China!" Seung-Hee disappeared. Half-way down, he popped his head out of the window. "Don't go away!"

The wind whistled around the tower and a low rumble of distant thunder momentarily covered the sound of heavy footsteps pounding down the tower steps. The young men burst from the doorway and onto the stone landing.

An explosive clap of thunder drew their eyes to the threatening sky. The stars and moon hid behind the swiftly moving clouds.

"The storm is coming. We have to go." The young men bowed and ran swiftly into the dark night.

Seung-Hee barely acknowledged his friends' good-byes, his attention focused on the travelers. He pinched his lips together, thinning his full lips into a straight line. His serious brown eyes studied Sabumnim, Jeffrey, and Charlotte. His black hair was pulled up and combed into a knot on top of his head and was bound with a band. He wore two hats; a round black hat covered by a bamboo reed hat. Pak Seung-Hee was the same height as Jeffrey but slightly huskier. The travelers waited, breathless. A slow smiled crossed Seung-Hee's face, and he bowed. He introduced himself to them.

"We've just begun trading with China. What can you tell me about them?"

A crack of thunder quickly followed a flash of brilliant lightning.

"Sabumnim, I want to go inside," Charlotte said nervously.

"Mr. Pak, may we stay in the observatory until the storm passes?" Sabumnim asked.

"I would be honored to offer my home as shelter," Seung-Hee said. "It's not far."

"Thank-you." Sabumnim bowed.

Jeffrey jogged down the path with Seung-Hee. "I was deep within China, in a monastery high in the mountains..."

# 10

# Wedding Preparations

"I was clinging by my fingernails to a huge stack of hemp some forty feet above the ground, when. . ."

Sabumnim cleared his throat. Jeffrey choked slightly on his words. "Well, high up anyway." He had to shout to be heard over the howling wind.

Seung-Hee chuckled.

A round-faced boy, about twelve years old and just beginning to lose his baby fat, rode a horse toward them. His dark hair, pulled back into a long single braid, was a striking contrast to the bright blue silk jacket he wore. He held onto the horse with one hand and with his other hand carefully clutched the box resting on his lap.

An older boy bent forward into the wind and led the horse. The wind whipped his short, silk jacket in the air. He held his narrow brimmed hat on his topknot.

The other boy fidgeted and accidentally kneed the horse in the ribs. The horse snorted and pranced forward. The older boy struggled to stay out of the horse's way and to keep his hat safe from the blustery wind.

Charlotte could have sworn the walking boy mumbled something sounding like, "Sit still! Now!"

They stopped by Pak Seung-Hee and the travelers.

"Good. We're not too late," Seung-Hee said.

He motioned everyone to stand back and pulled open a solid, wooden gate set in a high, stone wall. They entered a courtyard. Ahead of them was a whitewashed, one-story, U-shaped house with gray tiled roofs. The wall surrounded the house and courtyard.

The escort took the box from the boy and shouted, "Buy a box!"

Seung-Hee tried to take the box. The escort held it tightly and yelled again, "Buy a box!"

The boy on horseback watched, his eyes wide with interest.

At last, Seung-Hee motioned to the servants standing in the open doorway to bring food for the two. The escort turned the box over to Seung-Hee. Bowing, the boys left.

"The box holds clothes for my sister," Seung-Hee said. "She is getting married tomorrow to the boy on the horse."

"Married!" Jeffrey said. "He's younger than I am. No wonder he acted so squeamish!"

Seung-Hee stiffened. "My sister is very beautiful and only three years older than he is. Our families investigated the year, month, day, and hour of their births. According to these four pillars and the matchmaker, it's a very good match."

Jeffrey blushed. "I'm sorry. I only meant that in our country, we wait until we're older to get married, a lot older."

Seung-Hee thought for a minute. "Then you might be interested in our customs. Tomorrow we will have many guests, and you are welcome to stay and celebrate with us."

"Thank you," Jeffrey said, abashed.

With a final clap of thunder, rain spilled from the storm clouds.

They darted under the veranda formed by the eaves of the roof extending beyond the exterior walls. At the door, Seung-Hee removed his wooden shoes and waited for Sabumnim and the children to do the same.

Seung-Hee led them inside to a large room. The floor felt warm to their bare feet and was covered with heavy, oiled paper. A piece of silk embroidered with a wild crane hung on a wall. A chest with a blue dragon and a white tiger painted on it and two large, ceramic vases etched with lotus blossoms stood in a corner. A servant lit two oil lamps and brought in several square tables with very short legs.

"Come. I'll show you the kitchen since you're new here. It's right off the main room," Seung-Hee said.

An iron kettle simmered in the fireplace, which was dug on one side of the kitchen's hard dirt floor. A chimney ran from the fireplace straight up the wall. The center of the kitchen floor was sunken and the beams raised to increase the height of the room.

A woman bent over the kettle stirring the soup with a long-handled brass soup ladle. A beautiful teenager smiled at the newcomers, but particularly at Seung-Hee. She grasped the long handle of a bamboo strainer and moved it back and forth through the rice stored in a large, earthenware jar, sifting stones and sand out of the rice. She dropped the grains into an earthenware steamer on the fire and stirred the rice with a flat brass spoon and chopsticks.

Charlotte sniffed, enjoying the warm, spicy smells from the cooking food.

"They're cooking for tomorrow as well as dinner tonight. We'll have rice cakes at the celebration," Seung-Hee said.

They returned to the main room. Charlotte noticed two bamboo strainers hanging diagonally next to each other on a wall near the kitchen. Seeing her interest, Seung-Hee said, "They're for good fortune."

Doors covered with translucent paper slid open, and men and women talking animatedly but quietly to each other entered the room. The teenager from the kitchen joined them. Her black hair was parted in the center and pulled into a large knot at the back of her neck. She arranged her long, pale blue silk skirt and sat gracefully on one of the mats arranged around the tables. Seung-Hee sat next to her, with Jeffrey, Sabum-nim and Charlotte on his other side.

A plump, elderly man leaning on an elegantly carved cane entered the room. Charlotte noticed a flying crane embroidered on his long silk coat. Seung-Hee and the other men rose quickly. They knelt, bowed to the floor with their hands in front of them, rose and gave another quick bow. The women bowed from their sitting positions, placing their hands between their foreheads and the floor. Seung-Hee's father bowed and was seated at a spot farthest away from the door. The rest of the family returned to their seated positions.

"Why did everyone bow, Mr. Pak?" Charlotte whispered.

"Respecting our elders is a very important part of our Confucian beliefs. But we must not speak or even whisper while we are eating. Wait until dessert."

Servants brought in stoneware bowls of kimchee made of cabbage, onions, hot peppers and spices. Other covered bowls were filled with soup, rice, vegetables, and fish. To Charlotte's left, they placed a rice bowl and to her right, they set a soup bowl. She was given hot tea to drink.

Brass chopsticks as well as flat, oval shaped brass spoons were set in front of each person. Charlotte mused over her choices. She picked up her spoon and felt the curve in its handle. Then she put it down. Charlotte grasped her brass chopsticks and ate. She grinned triumphantly at Jeffrey.

When they finished, Seung-Hee turned to Sabumnim and the children. "I'll show you where you can rest." He rose, bowed to his father and slid open a door. Seung-Hee led the travelers down a hall.

Charlotte shared a room with Seung-Hee's sister, Bora, who looked a few years older than Jeffrey. Bora hadn't been at dinner. Charlotte noticed several bowls of half-eaten rice and kimchee placed on a low table. Next to them was a beautifully etched teapot. Several servants fussed busily about the girl.

Bora sat on a cushion in the middle of the room. A middle-aged woman wearing a servant's short, white jacket and wide trousers fussed over the young girl and painted her light skin a solid white. Charlotte unrolled her mat along one wall, sat cross-legged and watched.

"She's powdering my face for the wedding." Bora's cheek twitched. "It itches!" she whispered to Charlotte.

The servant turned her back, and Bora quickly scratched a spot by her right ear. Returning, the servant saw the streak left by Bora's fingernail. The older woman threw her hands up in the air.

"How am I going to make you look beautiful if you scratch it all off?"

Bora sat on her hands. Picking up the tiny bowl holding the powder, the servant returned to her task, all the while muttering to herself.

"We know you're getting married. We saw him outside," Charlotte said.

Bora's eyes brightened with curiosity. She leaned forward eagerly and bumped the woman's hand. The powder spilled. The old woman muttered louder. She put down the powder and picked up the hairbrush.

"We don't have time for this foolishness," she said sternly. "I must prepare you for your wedding tomorrow."

She loosened Bora's braid and brushed the shiny, dark brown hair, pulling it to a knot on top of her head. Hairs that were too short for the bun were plucked from Bora's head. The young girl blinked back tears.

"Ow!" Charlotte cringed.

Bora scrunched her mouth and rolled her eyes at the older woman. Charlotte nodded in sympathy with Bora. The older woman frowned.

Charlotte crawled to the paper door, slid it open and entered Jeffrey's and Sabumnim's sleeping area.

"Mr. Pak's sister is getting ready for her wedding. And it's not even until tomorrow!" Charlotte said.

"Girl stuff." Jeffrey smirked. He unrolled his mat. "Me? I'm going to like this. It's like camping, except the ground is warm and dry."

"That's because they have *ondol* heating." Sabumnim pointed to the small wood stove in the corner. "They build a fire in there and the heat runs under the floors through brick pipes. So they sit and sleep on warm floors."

They sat quietly for a few moments, listening to the rain and wind outside.

"Sabumnim, I forgot to show Jeffrey the game." Charlotte quickly crossed the floor to Jeffrey's mat. "Stand up, Jeffrey. Put one foot in front of the other. I'll give you a hint. This is a kick we do in class when I want to send you for a whirl." She stepped close to him and swept her leg forward and around his leg, catching the back of his ankle with her heel and knocking him off balance.

"You almost swept me off my feet. Oh! Sending me for a whirl. It's a *wuryo chagi*, a sweep kick." Jeffrey laughed.

"Tomorrow is a long day," Sabumnim interrupted.

"Okay." Charlotte paused. "I'll go watch that lady get Bora ready." She opened the door. "Good night." She slid the door closed behind her.

# 11

# Wedding Celebration

Sunlight filtered through opaque paper covered windows. Jeffrey awoke when Seung-Hee slid open their door.

"It's a beautiful day. Sunshine and blue sky. Hang up your mats and come to the main room. My new brother-in-law is arriving for the wedding and Bora will finally meet him. See you soon."

"Meet him? Don't they already know each other, Sabumnim?" Jeffrey rolled up his mat.

"No. Probably not. Mr. Pak talked yesterday about the match being good according to the stars. A matchmaker arranges marriages based upon the couple's dates of births and also on the way the marriage affects both families. The mother decides whether it's a good match for everyone. Bora will leave here today and live with her new husband's family."

Sabumnim placed his mat next to Jeffrey's. Rubbing her eyes, Charlotte shuffled into the room.

The three walked quietly down the hall to the main

room. At one end was a ten-paneled screen with pictures painted in fine, colorful detail on each panel. Charlotte noticed a crane like the one Seung-Hee's father had embroidered on his robe. This crane sat on a nest hidden in the middle of pine branches. A turtle graced one screen and a deer another. Pine trees and bamboo trees were painted on other screens.

Sabumnim pointed to four panels intermixed with the others. "See the sun, the clouds on that one, water over there and the rocks on the end screen? Those four common landscapes are often included on wedding screens."

"What's the mushroom stand for?" Jeffrey asked.

"It's the magic fungus. All of the panel symbols represent long-life and a crane at a wedding also stands for a happy marriage."

In front of the screen was a high table on which were placed a wooden mandarin duck, red and blue threads and candles.

"The mandarin duck represents a happy marriage and the threads represent longevity." Sabumnim looked over his shoulder. "The wedding's beginning. Let's stand over there."

The young groom walked on rice mats set out for the occasion to a mat in front of the decorated screen. His loose trousers were gathered at the ankles by colored bands and his long, flowing coat overlapped and tied with a single bow on his right side. A small red and green hat covered his topknot.

The bride wore a floor-length, red and green silk dress tied with a red sash. Her hair was covered with a jeweled headdress with an attached ten inch wide panel embroidered with gold thread which flowed down her back. She wore red silk shoes embroidered with colorful flowers.

The bride was slightly taller than the groom. They looked curiously at each other, bowed nervously and moved to opposite sides of a high table placed in front of the screen.

A woman entered the room with a bowl and a container of rice wine. After pouring wine into the bowl, she handed it to the groom to drink. His hands shook slightly. When he finished, the rest of the wine was given to the bride to drink. Bora's hands emerged from wide, flowing sleeves to take the wine. They repeated this process three times.

When the wedding ceremony was completed, the expressionless bride greeted her in-laws for the first time.

Charlotte, Sabumnim and Jeffrey trailed behind family members going outside to the inner courtyard.

"How come she didn't smile?" Charlotte asked.

"She's not smiling because of custom. If she smiles on her wedding day, all of her children will be girls," Sabumnim said.

Jeffrey snickered.

"So what's wrong with that?" Charlotte threw open one of the double wooden doors edged with iron and stomped through.

"She has a point." Sabumnim caught the flying door, and they went outside.

They found Charlotte and Seung-Hee standing by a three-foot sundial. The large inner courtyard was surrounded on three sides by the house and on the fourth by the tall, stone wall. Terraced, landscaped gardens within the courtyard provided quiet areas for reflection.

But at the moment, the courtyard hummed with the noise of men, women and children, all excitedly waiting for the celebration to start. They were dressed in their finest silks; the children wearing the most colorful clothing.

"I still can't believe how young the groom is," Jeffrey said.

"The woman I married is four years older than me," Seung-Hee said.

"You're married!"

"You must have noticed my topknot? Only unmarried boys and men wear long, braided pigtails. My wife sat next to me at dinner last night. Come. She is here somewhere. I will introduce you."

Seung-Hee ambled among noisy guests who were enjoying the activities and company. Speechless, Jeffrey followed. He didn't even notice men grunting and playing tug-of-war with a heavy rope made of straw or the young women laughing and taking turns on the courtyard swing. Still silent, he passed a zither musician who was attracting a large audience.

Charlotte and Sabumnim paused momentarily to listen. The musician's callused fingers plucked strings tightened on a flat board. The music of the strings sung in long and vibrating tones. Charlotte swayed in time to the rhythm.

Seung-Hee stopped beside the beautiful, delicately featured, young woman watching children crouching and jumping around a *yut nori* mat. When she smiled at Jeffrey, her cheeks creased into two dimples.

"Joo-Mi, remember our visitors?"

Joo-Mi bowed.

Jeffrey finally found his voice. "Pleased to meet you," he croaked. He waved across the courtyard. "Charlotte. Come meet Mr. Pak's wife."

Charlotte raced over. She recognized Joo-Mi from dinner. Joo-Mi patted an empty mat next to her, and Charlotte quickly sat down. Within a minute, she and Joo-Mi were deep in an animated conversation.

An excited screech from the game players caught the travelers' attention. A boy threw his four, wooden game sticks into the air and jumped back before the sticks landed on the mat.

"I have two flats!"

"Looks like a miniature baseball field," Jeffrey whispered to Charlotte.

She leaned closer to examine the sticks. They were flat on one side and rounded on the other sides.

Joo-Mi bent over and picked up a stick with her long, graceful fingers. "In yut nori," she said, "the more flats you throw, the more spaces you can move."

Men dressed in white baggy pants and jackets paraded past the yut nori game. One of the older boys stood and handed Charlotte his game pieces. "Here, you try." He swaggered after the men to the center of the courtyard.

Charlotte shrugged her shoulders. "Uh, okay."

Joo-Mi encouraged her. "Don't worry. You can do it."

Charlotte threw the yuts into the air with a loud kihap. Four flats fell on the center of the mat.

"She's on our team!" The boy's former teammates ran around Joo-Mi and pulled Charlotte over to their side. Charlotte giggled.

Seung-Hee, Sabumnim, and Jeffrey joined the growing crowd waiting for the exhibition to begin. The men in the center bowed and with a flurry of foot movements began their Taek Kyun demonstration. Each man demonstrated a technique he'd perfected.

Jeffrey was impressed with their speed and precision of movement. They came close to the swiftness shown by the best of the Hwarangdo fighters.

"I'm sorry. I must leave you now and check on my other guests," Seung-Hee said. "I have enjoyed our visit. Please stay as long as you can."

"Thank you for your hospitality," Sabumnim said.

Seung-Hee bowed.

"My kind of wedding," Jeffrey said, his attention once again on the demonstration. "Hey!" He felt a tug at his ankles. The shimmering blue ribbon tied itself around Jeffrey's and Sabumnim's legs. The ribbon's free end slithered along the ground toward the yut nori game, carefully avoiding Seung-Hee and his guests.

"I believe this time the ribbon wants to show us something," Sabumnim said.

Charlotte, waiting her turn, watched her new friends throw the sticks. The ribbon wrapped itself around her waist and misted.

# 12
## Koryo Dynasty

They landed on a secluded, grass lawn surrounded by a high wall. Far away, they could hear the sounds of a city; people and animals going about their daily business. But here, it was a green oasis, quiet and peaceful.

Young men, some in topknots and others with single braids, sat on their knees and wrote furiously at low tables. One young man stared blankly at the high, stone wall facing him and rocked silently back and forth, digging the toes of his black shoes into the ground. His eyes lit up. Abruptly, he stopped rocking. He removed a fine brush the size of a pencil from a jade-green porcelain holder. He briskly dripped water from the parrot shaped dropper into the powder on the yellow-green porcelain ink stone. He stroked his brush across the stone to mix the ink. He rapidly painted Chinese characters on the rice paper lying on the short legged table in front of him.

"What happened? Did I step on the ribbon?" Charlotte asked.

"No. The ribbon decided it was time to move on," Sabumnim said. "We're in the *Koryo* dynasty. They've developed celedon ware. That's the porcelain pieces you see. It's often praised as the finest ceramic in the world. The colors, especially the jade green pieces, are incredible."

One by one, the young men finished and handed their rice papers to one of several scribes kneeling near the wall. The scribes copied each paper, marked it with a fake name, made sure the ink was dry, rolled it and tossed it over the high stone wall.

"What in the world are they doing?" Jeffrey hooked his hands to the top of the wall, pulled himself up and watched.

Servants on the other side picked up the scrolls and handed them to a man sitting cross-legged on a thick mat under a maple tree. He wore a blue overcoat over his white, long-sleeved jacket and flowing trousers. The wings of the civil service hat fluttered gently in the breeze. He was surrounded by scrolls and a short, jade-green container holding brushes, the feathery bristle tips up.

He accepted the newest scroll and eagerly scanned the writing. He heard Jeffrey and looked up. The man glowered, and the tips of his long mustache wiggled. He crunched the scroll in his fist, leapt up and crossed the space between his mat and the wall with just a few quick strides.

"Show more self-control!" He bopped Jeffrey on the head with the scroll.

"Whoops!" Jeffrey dropped to the ground.

"This method of tossing the test over the wall is

supposed to prevent cheating," Sabumnim said. "These are rich, young aristocrats who were born to the class. They are forerunners of the yangban of the Yi dynasty. These men have studied for years at the government's National University, learning how to write poetry and studying Confucian classics in Chinese. You saw the Chinese symbols on the warehouse windows. The Koreans don't have their own written language yet. These men have to take the civil service exam for government jobs because there aren't enough jobs to go around."

"Can we look around?" Charlotte said.

Sabumnim agreed.

The three toured the city. Buddhist temples and pagodas abounded. The stone pagodas bore a softer look than the sleek, straight-lined ones built during the Shilla dynasty.

"They're impressive," Jeffrey said, "but they aren't carved as finely as the ones built during the Shilla dynasty."

"Many artisans are being attracted to Confucianism, and they aren't building pagodas as much. However, Buddhism is still strong during the Koryo dynasty," Sabumnim said. "In fact, because monasteries were tax exempt, the Buddhists became very wealthy. They raised livestock, sold products, established granaries and made wine."

Armed Buddhist monks marched by the travelers. Swords hung prominently at their sides.

Jeffrey excitedly tapped Sabumnim on the shoulder. "Did you see that? They're all armed and marching just like an army!"

"The monks have become so wealthy they need to protect their property, so they've trained monks as soldiers. They practice empty-hand fighting, too. And they've entered politics. The government sometimes uses Buddhist forces to put down trouble."

Men, women and children moved purposefully through the streets. A woman balancing a straw basket on her head walked gracefully by the travelers. Charlotte noticed a rounded bag made of knotted cord hanging around the woman's neck.

"It's a *chumoni*, a personal bag," Sabumnim said. "Since only men's vests had pockets, men and women wore these bags to carry things."

With a whoosh, the ribbon corralled Sabumnim and the children, cutting off their view. Its brilliant blue fabric grew in height with each new circle. Every fiber radiated strength and purpose as the ribbon whirled around and around.

Charlotte gaped at the ribbon imprisoning them. Its rapid movement encased them in their own little world. A section swirled close to her, inviting her to touch it. Hesitantly, she reached out, feeling the rich material slide under her fingers.

"Charlotte!" Jeffrey yelped. "Your hand!"

Charlotte stared. Her fingers had misted, turning into a shimmering shadow of flesh. She yanked her hand away from the ribbon; her fingers short stubs sticking out of her palm. Holding her breath, she watched the air above each finger waver and thicken, taking form. At last, her fingers reformed, and she heaved a sigh of relief. She felt them with her other hand.

"Not bad," Jeffrey said. "I'm going to try that." He leaned his head toward the ribbon.

Sabumnim laid a restraining hand on Jeffrey's shoulders and motioned him to sit down.

"The Koryo dynasty lasted from 918 to 1392 A.D." Sabumnim sat in the center and admired the ribbon's magnificence. "Under the leadership of Wang Kon, Taek Kyun grew and became an important part of military training. That is why the ribbon is so strong and beautiful now."

As suddenly as the ribbon rose and whirled, it slowed. Its upper edges wobbled and swayed wildly. The ribbon lost momentum and collapsed on top of them. For a brief second, disconnected arms and legs waved crazily in the air, then disappeared.

# 13

# The Mongol Invasion

Dropping the travelers onto a dirt roadway, the ribbon flashed the year 1232 A.D. and withdrew.

A frenzied mob: men, women, children and animals, charged the travelers.

"Look out!" Sabumnim pushed Charlotte and Jeffrey into a doorway.

"Run! To the ships! To the ships! They're coming! They're coming!" Hundreds of people thundered past them, shaking the building's walls.

A section of thatch fell off the roof, barely missing Jeffrey. He leaned forward for a better look. "Who's coming?"

Flailing arms struck Jeffrey and knocked him toward the street. Sabumnim grabbed Jeffrey before he became trampled by people bolting toward ships anchored in the harbor.

Servants carrying palanquins drove paths through the mob. Panting for breath, they bumped into anyone who didn't move fast enough to get out of their way.

The fabric covering the side of one palanquin flapped wildly and a man poked his head out. The

102

high-crowned black hat he wore had wings that came out on each side of his head, showing he was a member of the royal court.

The man slapped at the people pushing into the side of the chair. They grabbed the material and ripped off the entire side. The servant running behind, tangled his feet in the material and tripped.

The palanquin bounced, and the man inside hit his head on the wooden frame, squashing the top of his hat. He shouted angrily at the servants. They spurted ahead, bumping into a larger palanquin carried by four, muscled servants.

A baby cried in the large palanquin. Through the framed window, Jeffrey saw two women dressed in pastel colored silks screaming and picking themselves off the floor. Rivers of sweat dribbled down the servants' worried faces as they tried to keep the box steady.

In the street, a small child helped his mother drag an old chest behind them on two long poles. Her weathered face was creased with fear. The jostling mob pushed the woman aside, and she fell to the ground, cracking one of the poles. The chest tipped over into a deep mud hole. The child struggled weakly to pull it out of the mud.

An old man holding a kimchee pot close to his chest hobbled past them. "Run," he gasped. "The Mongols are coming!"

The woman pushed herself up and frantically threw open the chest. She rummaged for her steamer and wrapped it in a mat. She gave it to the child, picked up the three-year old and ran, leaving her other possessions behind.

Sabumnim took Charlotte's and Jeffrey's hands. "The Mongols! Hold on tight. We don't want to get separated in this mob." Seeing a slight opening, they lurched into the crowd.

Ships, ranging in sizes from family junks to larger cargo junks, jockeyed for the few places near the shore. Small junks carried people out to the larger ships. Other people waded and swam. A few lucky ships, already boarded with passengers, aimed for the open seas.

Charlotte looked to her right. Panic-stricken royalty and villagers fought each other for positions on a ship. Sailors, struggling to do their jobs, clashed with frightened people still trying to climb aboard. Some people were pulled off the side by others scrambling over them. The overloaded and off-balance ship tipped, pitching passengers into the churning water. Terrified people swam for safety, only to find themselves back on dry land with all of the others fleeing the invading Mongols.

Sabumnim, Jeffrey, and Charlotte dashed onto a small junk. Within seconds, it was filled. With long bamboo poles, two sailors pushed the junk through the shallow water to a larger ship further out.

Once at the ship, the passengers swarmed over the sides. Sabumnim found a spot for the three of them to crawl up. Others rapidly followed Sabumnim's lead. The three were pushed to the center of the ship.

"That's all we can hold." The captain motioned to set sail.

"Where are we going? Why did we run?"Charlotte pushed away a man and a woman who were crowding too close.

The billowing sails caught the wind and snapped taut. The creaking ship sailed effortlessly through small swells.

Clouds of dust appeared on the horizon, moving ever closer to the city. The people scattered. Some sprinted for the mountains; others hid in abandoned buildings.

Fierce looking men wearing hooded leather and metal coats galloped on horseback down to the river's edge. They pulled arrows from quivers on their backs, drew their bows and aimed. Deadly arrows peppered the stern of the slowest ship. The Mongol soldiers arced their bows and shot a second round. The arrows fell harmlessly into the water.

"They'll go to sea after us!" Jeffrey pointed to a few remaining ships in the harbor.

"No, they won't. Even though the Mongols are vicious fighting men and have conquered Russia, China, Persia and our country, they won't come after us. They are afraid of the water," another passenger said. The ship rolled with a large swell. The passenger tightened his grip on the railing and bent his legs to roll with the movement. "Most of the city is escaping to the island across the river. Others in the country are seeking safety in walled cities in the mountains."

Unable to reach the sailing ships with their arrows, the armored horsemen torched the docked ships and rode into the city in search of remaining villagers.

Next to Sabumnim, a man dressed in silk and the winged hat of the royal court spoke. "Look at that." He pulled thoughtfully on his beard. "We can train our archers to fight from horseback. They could use crossbows or short reflex bows and the quiver could be kept on the soldier or on the horse. We could have our own mobile army."

The wild, rolling sea tossed the ship, smacking Sabumnim, Jeffrey, and Charlotte back and forth into each other and the other passengers. The wooden ship groaned. Gulls screeched high overhead. Passengers shoved each other for more space.

"Ugh." Charlotte held her stomach. "I can't breathe."

Sabumnim lifted her above the crowd for a breath of fresh air.

Spotting the ribbon flapping in the wind as part of the sail, Charlotte spread her fingers and reached for it.

"Beach!"

# 14
## Pirates

They splashed into knee-deep water and were knocked over by a wave slapping into them from behind.

Jeffrey rose, water dripping from his dobok and hair. "Next time say island, Charlotte. Island!"

Charlotte sniffed. She pulled up her slipping pants and waded ashore to the sandy beach.

"There's only one ship. Where are the others?" Jeffrey looked back at the calm sea.

"The ribbon says we've traveled almost fifty years." Sabumnim wrung water from his sleeve. "The people we set sail with have settled, raised families, and grown old here. Despite the people's escape, the Mongols are in control of Korea, even the islands."

Charlotte dug the toes of her shoes into the warm sand and gazed toward the land. "It looks like steps are dug into the hillside."

"Those are terraced rice paddies," Sabumnim said. "The green area is filled with rice seedlings which are ready to be transplanted into the steps. It'll be a lot of work."

They walked toward the hillside and clambered upwards, finally finding a farmer's worn path. The three climbed higher up the hillside, leaving the paddies far behind them.

The path became narrower and less traveled. Charlotte stepped over larger and larger rocks. The rolling hillside disappeared, becoming a wilder, rockier cliff.

Voices drifted down from high above them. "I tell you it's time! If it isn't the Mongols taxing us and taking our grain, then it is our king. If I were of royal blood, I'd send my children off to marry Mongol princesses and princes and live in China too. Instead, they take my oldest son to die on their battlefield. And my younger sons and their families are starving with me on the farm."

The voices grew louder as the path turned toward them.

"But, brother, it's not honorable to be a thief."

"Selling yourself and your family into slavery just so you don't have to pay taxes isn't honorable either. I'd rather join the Japanese wako. Yes. You heard me. The pirates. I can guide them to many riches and inland cities. And I'll have food to eat." The man's voice became low and threatening. "And no one is to know I've done so. It'll be death to anyone who finds out what I'm doing. They're here now. That's their ship in the harbor. This is my chance to join them."

"I think we should go." Sabumnim reached for the ribbon.

The ribbon shook, giving the illusion of chuckling. It curled out of reach and blended into the light blue of the sky.

The voices came closer. "Please, brother. I beg you. These pirates are dangerous and desperate men. They steal anything to survive. They live by hit and run raids, and we suffer."

"I'm desperate, too. I'm not going to be pushed around anymore. It's my turn to push others."

"Quick. This way." Sabumnim chose an offshoot of their path. The new path led inland and upward through the increasingly desolate, craggy cliffs.

"I have made my choice." The angry voices were right behind them on the path.

"They're following us," Jeffrey said.

Sabumnim picked up the pace. The travelers passed charred remains of trees and brush.

"They must have had a major fire," Jeffrey said.

"The Koreans destroyed the trees to add to the barren look of the coastline and discourage invaders," Sabumnim said.

The rugged path twisted and turned, always leading upwards and away from the coast. Maple trees cast out low, leafy branches and the underbrush grew more lush.

A mile further, the path took a rocky turn. The air became thinner the higher they climbed. It was harder to breathe, especially moving as fast as they were. One side of the path rose hundreds of feet up an irregular rock face. Colorful purple and yellow flowers blossomed in the rock's cracks. The other side of the path fell over a hundred feet into a gorge.

Charlotte could hear a low rumbling in the distance. The rocky path curved out of sight and the rumbling grew louder.

Their path ended. A thunderous waterfall pounded down the cliff and blocked the trail. Its glistening layers of foam shot out of the rock a hundred feet above them and disappeared into the gorge below.

"We can't go back," Jeffrey yelled above the roar. "And they're not that far behind. There's got to be a way across."

He climbed down over boulders made slippery from the waterfall's wide flung spray. Following Jeffrey, Charlotte and Sabumnim scrambled over the rocks.

Jeffrey slid off the last boulder and onto a level place lower than the original path. He surprised a red fox drinking from a puddle. The fox darted into the darkness behind the fall.

"There's an opening behind the fall!"

Sabumnim entered.

The sun, sparkling off the shimmering veil of water, threw hundreds of rainbows. Momentarily distracted, Charlotte stared at the constantly changing colors. Then she looked behind her.

"Keep going!" She pushed ahead of Jeffrey and entered the damp cave. The treacherous, unending crystal sheet of water rushed within a few feet of them.

Bursting into the bright sunshine on the other side, they closed their eyes against the glare. The rocky path was high above them. Sabumnim leapt for a hold, and grasping the rim with his fingertips, he pulled himself up to the path.

"Give me your hand." He laid on the path and lowered his arms.

Jeffrey jumped, stretching for Sabumnim's fingertips and missed, slipping on the damp boulders. He snatched at a jagged rock and stopped himself from falling feet into the gorge. Eyes squeezed shut, he hugged the rock for a few moments and controlled his breathing.

Jeffrey pulled himself up. He saw Sabumnim glancing worriedly at him. Jeffrey smiled shakily. "We'll find a better spot." He waved vaguely at a point further along the rocks.

Sabumnim checked their back trail. There was no sign of the brothers. He nodded to Jeffrey and walked above them, watching Jeffrey and Charlotte carefully test each rock for stability before clambering over it. Far below, the white-water rapids rushed along the bottom of the gorge.

An ancient pine tree, held only by a few remaining roots, jutted upwards from the mountainside. Jeffrey grabbed a root dangling from the trunk and pulled several times to test it. He inhaled deeply and firmly gripped the root. Hand over hand, he pulled himself up. The root thickened, and Jeffrey's grip loosened. He slipped and caught himself again. He hung in mid-air, too far away to reach the trunk or the cliff wall.

Charlotte jumped to the rock just below Jeffrey, grabbed his ankles and swung them. Jeffrey shot forward, then backwards, just missing Charlotte who hastily ducked. Jeffrey bent his knees and thrust his feet forward and upward, finding a foothold higher up the rocky wall. He grasped another root closer to the cliff and pulled his body onto the roots still clinging to the mountainside.

He gingerly stepped from one exposed root to another until he reached the trunk. It held his weight.

He lay flat and hugged the trunk. He wiggled a loose root in front of Charlotte. She gripped the end and wrapped it around her wrist. Jeffrey sat up and pulled Charlotte up. At last, she was close enough to the trunk to grasp the rough bark and climb. The tree trembled and creaked under her added weight. Jeffrey boosted her up to Sabumnim.

The ground around the roots loosened, sending large chunks of dirt and rocks tumbling down the mountainside. Smaller roots snapped free of the earth and the trunk dropped several inches. Jeffrey flopped backwards and was caught in the arms of the broken branches. Only the main root connected the old pine to solid earth.

"Hurry, Jeffrey!" Charlotte bit her lip.

Jeffrey slowly unbent his body, section by section until he stood. He took two steps. The tree swayed. Jeffrey bent his legs, pushed off the trunk and jumped, catching the edge of the path with his forearms. Sabumnim grasped Jeffrey's shoulders and helped him up.

The ground cracked and split beneath them. The three sprang for safety. The main root ripped out of the mountainside, taking boulders and a wide section of the path with it. The ancient, dead pine bounced end over end into the gorge.

They looked at each other and nervously chuckled. "Whew. That was close."

With the path behind them torn away there was only one direction to go and no way for the farmer turning pirate to run into them. They relaxed, taking time to admire the blue sky and wispy clouds above and the narrow river twisting along the canyon's bottom.

The trail narrowed to a foot-wide ledge. They were forced to walk single-file. Sabumnim disappeared around a sharp corner. Jeffrey and Charlotte pressed their backs to the cliff and slowly side-stepped after Sabumnim.

The path gradually widened and wound away from the canyon, allowing the travelers to hike side by side. Birds twittered and flew overhead. Thick bushes, dwarf pines, and leafy maples formed a serene forest glade. The undergrowth rustled and two rabbits hopped away.

Sabumnim halted abruptly at a clearing. Charlotte, who had been watching the rabbits, bumped into him. She peered around him and stiffened. The three gaped at a tattered group of pirates practicing sword fighting.

A man, his face scarred with old wounds, stood on a broad rock. He twisted his dark, straight beard and closely observed the combat. His white jacket hung open, and he had rolled his dirt streaked trousers up to his knees. A fly landed on a sweaty knee. He absentmindedly scratched it off with his other foot. He appeared to be the leader.

One of the barefoot fighters knocked his opponent's sword out of his hands. The swordless man scuttled out of reach. The broad-shouldered man gripped his sword with two strong hands and eyed the leader.

The scarred man's shoulders tensed, and he lowered his hand to his side. He flexed his knees and bent slightly, positioning his weight evenly on both feet. His eyes narrowed. He growled.

The broad shouldered man smirked and slashed his sword from side to side. It whipped through the air. He charged the man on the rock. The man jumped, bent his shoulder and rolled, knocking the bandit off his feet. The sword flew from the pirate's hands. The leader scrambled to his feet and picked up the sword.

The downed man stood and sputtered. He faced the leader who motioned with the sword to go up on the rock. The pirate climbed to the top and thumped himself on the chest. He shouted, jumped off the rock, and landed flat on his stomach. The others laughed and jeered.

"Roll, you fool. Bend your shoulder under you." The leader demonstrated.

"The pirates," Jeffrey whispered.

Charlotte clutched Sabumnim's leg, her body frozen in fear.

All movement stopped at the sound of Jeffrey's voice. The pirates' faces turned cold and threatening. They drew their swords. The leader threw the sword back to the broad shouldered pirate who caught it easily.

"Run!" Sabumnim peeled Charlotte from his leg and took an arm. Jeffrey grabbed her other arm.

They darted back the way they had come, ducking under low-hanging branches. Dodging and weaving down the path, they carried Charlotte, still frozen, between them.

They barely slowed their pace when they reached the narrow cliff path. Charlotte's feet swung out and over the edge.

Swinging back over the path, Charlotte began to breathe again. She bicycled the air, her feet too high to touch the ground. "Faster!"

The pirates stormed after them, tripping over each other in their furious race to be the first to reach the intruders.

"But," a brother yelled over the waterfall's rumble, "what about our family's honor?"

Sabumnim and Jeffrey screeched to a halt at the fresh, deep gouge torn by the fallen tree. Jeffrey's foot skidded into the ditch. Loose stones bounced noisily into the hole and over the jagged edge of the cliff and finally landed with a soundless splash in the river at the bottom of the gorge. Jeffrey jerked his foot back.

Sabumnim looked over his shoulder. Angry footsteps pounded the path behind them, moving ever closer.

Charlotte uncurled her legs; her feet touched the ground. She shrugged off their hands. "Sabumnim, the ribbon is back!"

Part of the pale blue ribbon was caught above them on an uneven, rocky overhang. The rest of the ribbon hung away from the ledge and fell past them into the yawning canyon.

Jeffrey tried to snag the ribbon with his long arms. "We'll never be able to reach it, Sabumnim."

Sabumnim glanced back; the wako turned the corner. On the other side of the newly formed gash stood the two brothers. One brother drew an ancient sword menacingly from its scabbard.

The ribbon fluttered in the gentle breeze.

"Sometimes you have to work with what you have at the moment," Sabumnim said.

The three nodded at each other and sprang toward the ribbon.

# 15

# General Yi's Revolt

A steady rain washed away the mist. Sabumnim stood on a grassy hill with Charlotte and Jeffrey lying on the ground still clinging to Sabumnim's black belt. The ribbon, thinned to half its normal width, trailed miserably down the hill.

At the foot of the hill, embedded in mud, lay a large army camp. Muddy tents, drenched from heavy rains, sagged limply. Banners and flags drooped from their poles. An ox strained to pull a wagon through the camp. The iron wheels gouged the soaked earth, leaving deep wagon ruts. Smoke from cooking pits fought to rise against the cold rain blowing in under makeshift shelters. A few soldiers pushed for space closest to the weak flames and warmed their hands.

A sentry, keeping a half-hearted watch, pulled his wet, thickly padded jacket away from his body. A lone soldier addressed the sentry. The sentry lifted the flap of his helmet away from his ear, spoke to the soldier and pointed to a large tent. The soldier ignored the sentry and trudged past him toward the river. The bored sentry leaned against a post and watched.

Cannons, mired in the mud, formed a haphazard line along the river bank. None of the cannons pointed across the river at the enemy camp.

The soldier stood in front of the largest cannon. He took a deep breath and encircled the barrel with his arms. He struggled to direct it toward the Chinese fort across the river, but the cannon was too heavy. The soldier lost his footing and slid through the mud. He instinctively gripped the cannon's barrel and avoided sitting in the muck.

The soldier regained his footing and struck the cannon barrel with his fist, breaking through the rusty metal. He wrapped his bleeding hand in the bottom half of his jacket.

The soldier wiped the rain off his forehead and turned toward the enemy which he could barely see across the wide river. Fresh troops and wagon loads of supplies pulled by fresh teams of oxen plowed through the mud to the front gate of the fort.

The soldier kicked the cannon. A piece fell off. His shoulders slumped in defeat, and he waded through the mud toward the large tent. Deep lines of despair aged his face.

Around the camp, soldiers raised soggy tent flaps and slogged toward the large tent.

"Something's going to happen." Jeffrey followed the ribbon to the brink of the hill.

Charging up the hill, the soldiers knocked Jeffrey flat.

Sabumnim stepped forward. He flipped a soldier who was about to run over Charlotte and threw him to the ground. The next man lunged toward Sabumnim. Sabumnim clutched the man's arms, put his foot into the soldier's stomach, and dropped to the ground. Rolling backwards, he tossed the soldier who did a somersault over Sabumnim's head and landed with a splat in the wet grass. Sabumnim bounded to his feet. The flow of soldiers parted around the trio and rushed down the other side of the hill.

Sabumnim helped Jeffrey to his feet. "Deserters. Stay close."

"Like gum on your sneakers."

Soldiers filed into the main tent and waited restlessly for their general to appear.

"We'll wait until everyone enters," Sabumnim said.

The travelers stopped next to a small tent. Voices drifted through the openings.

"I had a dream, Priest Muhak," a deep voice said. "In it, I was trying to rest but I was lying over three logs. It was extremely uncomfortable. I think it's a bad omen. I need to know for sure before I take my next step."

"Don't worry, General Yi," the priest said. "It's a good sign but with a few drawbacks. Your body across three logs forms the Chinese character for king. But it'll be an uncomfortable reign because of the in-fighting between your sons."

"So it's a good sign. I will be king." The other spoke softly. "Thank you, Muhak. You can go now."

A Buddhist priest left the tent soon followed by General Yi, a man in his early fifties. He was dressed in full body armor and wore the pointed helmet favored by the cavalry. He strode purposefully to the large tent and entered.

Sabumnim and the children squeezed into the back of the tent.

General Yi Song-gye was a fiery man. He stood at the front of his silent, disgruntled troops. His dark eyes seemed to pierce through each and every man.

"I've made my decision," he said. "We've been struck by desertion and disease. These past months of unending rain and lack of supplies have made our orders to attack the Chinese fort across the river impossible.

"I have never been in favor of fighting the Chinese. Our country has successfully run off the Mongols, but it is our government's poor decisions that have brought us to this humiliating point." He paused, then thundered. "Our government is the real enemy. It must go! We leave for Kaesong tonight!"

"Kaesong! Kaesong!" The troops slapped each others' backs and triumphantly raised their swords high.

The ribbon twitched beneath Sabumnim's feet. He motioned to the children and followed the ribbon outside. Within a few feet of the tent, it sunk into the slick mud.

Jeffrey tried to dig it out of the thick goo.

"Careful. The way it has narrowed, there's no telling what effect it will have on our travels," Sabumnim said.

"But I want to see General Yi lead his troops."

"We can try. Kaesong, 1388."

Mud splattered everywhere as the mist rose.

# 16
# Founder Yi's Reforms

"As part of the reform, our great Founder Yi has proclaimed our land will again be known by the ancient,
beautiful name of Choson."

The three travelers had landed in the back of a classroom. The floor was covered by heavy, oiled paper just
like in Pak Seung Hee's home. The walls were covered
with rice paper.

The teacher sat cross-legged on a cushion in
front of his class. He wore a white jacket
which tied on one side and white trousers
and white shoes. His beard and mustache
were dark brown, and he wore a three
layered hat over his topknot. Each
layer of his hat winged upwards, the
next one narrower than the one below
it. The teacher held a bamboo stick
which he stamped on the ground
to emphasize what he said. He
pointed to a student to read.

The students, all boys, knelt on the floor with their hands on their knees and studied books placed in front of them. A boy used a pointer stick to read the characters out loud. One boy, about eight years old, wiggled closer to the paper wall behind him. He scratched the paper with a fingernail and poked a hole in it. When that was accomplished, he stole a quick look at his teacher. He was talking to another student. The boy bent over and looked through the hole. The bamboo rod landed on his shoulder. The boy yelped.

"Pay attention."

"This isn't a battle. This is school!" Jeffrey folded his arms and sulked.

Startled, the teacher glared sternly at Sabumnim, Charlotte, and Jeffrey. "You must know that females are not allowed in the same room as males and definitely not in a classroom."

The students' long braids flipped over their shoulders as they turned to look curiously at the newcomers.

Sabumnim rose and bowed. The three walked outside and sat on a stone bench placed under a shady walnut tree.

"No girls in the same room with boys?" Jeffrey flicked Charlotte's ponytail. "Not a bad idea."

"A lot has happened since Bora's wedding. When the Mongols ruled, Koreans kept women behind high walls for protection. In the later years of the Yi dynasty, Neo-Confucianism became popular. It clearly stated what men's roles were and what women could do. Boys and girls over the age of seven couldn't be in the same room anymore. It wasn't considered proper behavior. A few hundred years from now, women must cover their faces to go outside. Upper class women were only allowed outside late in the evening when all the men were inside."

Many men and a few women passed by their bench. Two men deep in conversation paused in front of them. One was richly dressed in blue and green silks; the other wore a pale blue vest with pockets over his jacket and wide trousers drawn tight at the waist. Charlotte slyly touched the vest.

"Sabumnim." She whispered behind her hand. "The clothes look the same, but the material is soft."

"They no longer use hemp to make most of their clothes. They use cotton. The Koreans invented a cotton gin and a spinning wheel and began purchasing cotton from China. The rich aristocrats still use silks and ramie cloth."

The civil servant in cotton was trying to calm the rich man.

"I'm not going to let you take everything." The rich man spoke through clenched teeth.

"Sir, there's nothing I can do," the official said.

"Just because the land was given to my father and he died, I'm losing my inheritance instead of gaining it. People have always inherited land."

"This is a part of Founder Yi's reform. You must now be a public office-holding yangban to receive and keep land from the government. Not just a former official or a son of a former official. My yangban boss is one of those working on the *Confucian* beliefs that will govern us."

"But I'm not of that class, and I didn't pass the state examination. I'm reduced to working someone's farm for wages. Me!"

The official bowed. "I'm sorry, Sir. There's nothing I can do." He left the man standing in the middle of the road.

The former landowner trudged down the street, the heels of his shoes grinding the faded ribbon deeply into the dirt road.

"The ribbon's so dirty. Will we be able to travel on it?" Charlotte flicked off the bigger lumps of dirt.

"The way the ribbon's been working we'll probably wind up back at Taekwondo class." Jeffrey pitched a clump of mud at the walnut tree. It stuck to the bark, a blot shaped like a tarantula which slowly broke apart and slithered down the trunk.

"You must learn to deal with each adventure as it happens." Sabumnim smoothed a few wrinkles out of the fabric.

Jeffrey sighed.

While they cleared the dirt from the ribbon, it flashed them ahead.

# 17
# City Life

Sabumnim and the children found themselves sitting on a wide stone wall. Where they sat, the granite bricks joined together perfectly and formed a flat top. Further along the wall, the bricks formed an A-shaped roof. The travelers' feet disappeared into a swirling, shifting mist as thick as whipped cream.

"This isn't class, and it's probably not Kaesong either." Jeffrey looked up at the snow covered mountains poking out of the mist. He stood. "I'm going to look around." Jeffrey started to step off the wall.

"Wait." Sabumnim caught Jeffrey's arm and motioned him to sit down again. "You must always be aware of your surroundings."

Slowly the mist lowered, exposing sections of stone wall, layer by layer, until the ground appeared more than twenty feet below them.

Jeffrey's eyes widened into large Os. "That would have been some step! But why would someone build a wall around mountains?"

"They didn't. There's a city further down on this side of the wall," Charlotte said.

Jeffrey looked over his shoulder.

"It must be *Hanyang*. Later they'll call it *Seoul*." Sabumnim rose. "General Yi moved the capital here and built this wall to keep the invaders out. He asked Muhak, the Buddhist priest, to select the site of the new capital city and design it."

Ahead of them, towering above the wall, rose two broad, rectangular roofs, one on top of the other. Thick columns supported the space in-between.

"Maybe it's part of the palace. Let's go visit General Yi. He can tell me about the battle." Jeffrey marched along the top of the wall which curved and twisted, following the ups and downs of the mountainside.

The massive, pagoda style roof appeared. It was the top part of an elaborate gate which led through the wall and into the city. The thick doors were just being opened for the day's business.

The travelers entered the gallery under the first roof. From there they could look out over the dirt streets below. A few of the main streets were straight.

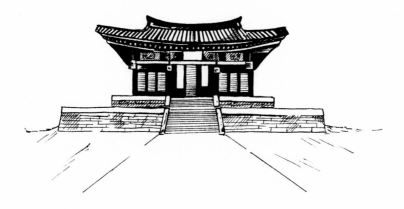

Branching off the main streets were many twisting side streets.

Within the city wall were many houses and compounds. Each compound held a large U-shaped house, several smaller huts and an inner courtyard surrounded by a high stone wall.

"Yangban live in the compounds," Sabumnim said. "The middle class, which includes doctors and lower government officials, live over there in the two and three-room houses covered by tile."

Rows upon rows of one-storied houses constructed of mud bricks and covered with thatch were squashed together next to the city wall. Narrow, crooked streets separated some of the buildings.

"Many servants who don't live in the compounds live in those poorer huts."

"It's all so, so brown," Charlotte said. "Almost everything I see is brown. Brown streets, tan thatched roofs, mud walls, and brownish-blue tiles."

Not too far away, they could see a tall many storied palace. The eaves were colorfully painted.

"The only thing that's colorful is the king's palace," Jeffrey said. "Don't people paint their houses?"

"It's considered bad taste and an invitation to thieves to show how well off you are. Most people keep the front of their houses plain. Behind the false fronts of the large compounds are gracious homes," Sabumnim said.

Jeffrey hurried ahead toward the palace.

It was early morning. Charlotte pulled Sabumnim's sleeve and pointed. Two young girls hiding behind a tree in a walled courtyard watched an elderly, well-dressed man leave the house. The inner courtyard was landscaped with lotus ponds, grassy lawns, trees and bushes. Servants opened the heavy gates for the man and closed them carefully behind him.

He stepped into a chair which resembled an open carriage. A tall, wooden frame on the back and front allowed two servants to lift the chair by poles balanced on their shoulders. Two other servants held two long poles underneath the carriage. Every few minutes they would lift those poles, lessening the weight on the shoulders of the other two.

The girls scampered to a seesaw placed next to the wall. They balanced on both ends and took turns jumping up and stealing peeks over the wall to watch the man and servants leave. The man ignored girls from other courtyards bouncing up and craning their necks to watch him.

Sabumnim and Charlotte walked along the top of the wall. Sabumnim caught sight of a man walking briskly along a narrow, winding street near the city wall. He stopped before one of many adobe buildings with gray tiled roofs. Its lattice work windows and doors were covered by thick, opaque rice paper and hinged at the top. The man lifted the bottoms of the door and windows and hooked them under the eaves. He removed his shoes and entered the building. The cool morning breeze flowing through the raised door and windows fluttered the hems of his wide trousers.

The man struggled to lift a heavy, wooden box from a shelf and dropped it at the edge of a large, wooden press table. He selected metal blocks from the box and pounded them into a wide frame on the table. Then he lifted down a covered ceramic bowl holding ink. After reading the type one more time, he rapidly replaced a few pieces and nodded in satisfaction.

The man reached for a sheet of mulberry paper and bumped the box of metal blocks which teetered on the table's edge. The blocks shifted inside the box, and the box crashed to the floor, scattering metal type. A few rolled outside.

"That looks like a four." Charlotte knelt and pointed to a cube lying at the bottom of their wall. "And that looks like a man with a hat, and that's two lines with a squiggle."

"It's an early print shop," Sabumnim said. "The printing press existed in Korea about thirty-eight years before it appeared in Europe."

"Is that Chinese writing?"

"Since we're in the 1400s, you're looking at Korea's written language, Hangul. Women and commoners were pleased when it was created because it was easier for them to learn to read and write their own language than Chinese. The rich men looked down on it."

"Hurry up!" Jeffrey marched toward the palace.

Catching up, they saw the towering building wasn't a palace, nor was it enclosed by the city wall. It was a Buddhist temple located outside the city walls. Holes and cracks marred many of the green tiles covering the roofs. The colorful paintings on the eaves were faded and streaked with dirt.

The temple was abandoned. A once majestic statue of Buddha lay shattered near the front gate. Stone benches, covered with fungus, lay pitted and broken in the temple courtyard.

Small, beady eyes peered at them from behind the chipped columns of the first story. The rats squealed and backed into the darkness as Sabumnim, Jeffrey and Charlotte approached. The rats kept a steady watch from deep within the temple.

"What happened to the monks?" Jeffrey asked.

"This is one result of the reforms of the Yi dynasty. The General Yi we met earlier has been dead for years. This is the time of the fourth ruler, Sejong the Great. When General Yi became Yi Taejo, the first ruler of the Yi dynasty, he followed only part of Priest Muhak's advice about building Seoul. When it came to putting a Buddhist temple inside the walls, Yi Taejo listened to a Confucian scholar instead."

A large, fat rat poked his nose out the doorway of the pagoda and strolled across the empty courtyard.

"The Yi dynasty blamed the Buddhists for the Mongol invasion and for corrupting the Koryo government. The government closed the temples and the monks fled to the mountains. If a Buddhist monk entered the city, he was killed. The government followed Confucianism, and in addition to the already strict Confucian code, the dynasty set up more rules and outlawed new ideas and ways of doing things."

"So in with the old and out with the new?" Jeffrey asked.

"There were still some new ideas. Let's find the ribbon, and I'll show you a forerunner to the submarine."

# 18
## Turtle Boats

A steady clang of hammers echoed off the walls of a foundry. Charlotte covered her ears. Steam rose from a large kettle filled with fiery, glowing red-orange liquid. Beads of sweat gathered on Jeffrey's forehead. The men turned the kettle and poured the liquid down a tube and into a mold.

Sabumnim pointed. Further down, men hammered open cooled molds and drew out large pointed spikes. They cleaned the surfaces and attached them to thick, six-sided wooden blocks. More men fastened the spiked blocks together.

"Sabumnim, that's starting to look just like a turtle shell," Jeffrey said.

"That's what they were called, turtle boats or *ko-bukson*. They're one of Admiral Yi Sun-Sin's many inventions."

Several men surrounded a heavy, spiked section. They bent their knees, grunted, and lifted. The men carried it outside into the bright sunlight.

Sabumnim and the children followed. Using ropes

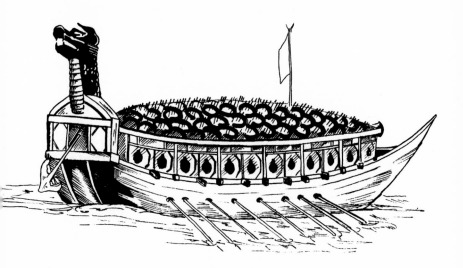

and pulleys, the workers raised the new piece and attached it to the top of a galley boat. The boat was a hundred and ten feet long and twenty-eight feet wide.

Rising straight up from the front of the boat was a long, fat neck with a head on it.

"It looks like an angry porcupine with a turtle head," Charlotte said.

Men bustled about the busy wharf. Many wore white, long-sleeved jackets tied at the chest or waist with belts. Their wide bottomed trousers were bound at the ankles, and they wore leather shoes. Most wore topknots and only a few were hatless.

Twelve turtle boats, including the one just completed, were pulled close to the shore and anchored by ropes tied to iron hooks on the wharf. Smaller boats transported supplies to the turtle boats. The men climbed rope ladders to the turtle boats, loading supplies in the cabins and bottom deck. Boxes loaded with cannon balls, gunpowder, and the mineral, saltpeter, were pulled up the side of the boat by ropes and pulleys. Arrows, wood, and boxes containing small yellow chunks were passed upwards by the human chain of men standing on ladders.

A man, his sleeves rolled up, stood on the spiked deck and shouted to the men below. They sent a basket of dried grass and straw up to him.

"Why are they thatching the boat's roof?" Jeffrey asked.

"The straw hides the spikes from an enemy trying to board the ship."

Below the iron spiked roof, thirty-six copper cannons poked out of narrow slits in the sides of the upper deck. Four additional cannons divided between the front and back protected the ship from attacks in those directions.

"The boats can fire in any direction!" Jeffrey said.

A man waved arrows through one of the upper holes on the side of a ship. More arrows were sent up to him.

Oars sprouted from the middle of the ship, ten on each side. A tall mast rose from the center of the turtle boat. Some boats already had their sails hoisted.

A gong called for attention. The ribbon wrapped its shiny folds around it. The date on the ribbon was 1598 A.D. Fighting men, wearing helmets and armor netting resembling loosely woven dresses of fish scales, gathered around the gong. Long sabers bounced at their sides.

Everyone turned toward the lead turtle boat. In front of it, an imposing man, much taller than the other Koreans on the dock, held his helmet in his hand while he talked to the men. He was dressed for battle.

"I can't hear," Charlotte said, disappointed.

Sabumnim leaned toward the speaker and repeated the main points of Admiral Yi's speech.

"He's saying," Sabumnim said, "that for six years, the Japanese, under the rule of Shogun Hideyoshi, have invaded Korea, destroying buildings, books, and farm lands."

Sabumnim listened intently for a few minutes. "He's explaining that with the help of the Chinese navy, their goal is to destroy the rest of the Japanese fleet as it leaves Korea so the Japanese can't come back. The Koreans will use a fishnet approach to trap the ships. Now he's saying that even though the Hwarangdo have fallen out of favor with the Yi dynasty, the men must remember the Hwarangdo code of honor."

"I know the code!" Charlotte said.

"Admiral Yi lives and fights by it."

A cheer rose from the crowd.

"He's just ordered them to battle!"

Admiral Yi Sun-Sin placed his helmet on his head and entered his boat. The fighters sprinted for the boats which would take them to the turtle boats.

"Where are the rest of my rowers?" A captain yelled from an open hatch.

"We're right here!" Jeffrey jumped into a boat waiting to take rowers to the larger boats.

Charlotte raced after him.

"Jeffrey! Charlotte! They're going into battle!"

"I'm not going to lose him again." She scrambled into the boat which immediately left the dock.

"We're not going into battle!" Sabumnim jumped into the remaining boat going out to the ships.

Jeffrey and Charlotte climbed the swaying ladder and slipped through the open hatch into the dimly lit interior. Sabumnim entered another hatch on the same boat. The hatches were closed and locked after them.

Seamen hoisted the square sail through the narrow center slot.

A seaman ordered Sabumnim to the lower level, and he found a place next to Charlotte on a rowing bench. He sighed. They grasped the ends of a long, slender wooden oar and waited.

"Row port." The middle-aged seaman took his orders from the upper level.

"Is that our side?" Jeffrey sat behind Sabumnim and Charlotte.

The ship set sail. A man sitting at a large drum struck a regular rhythm for the rowers to follow.

A cannon blast rung in the distance, followed by a swirling whistle arcing toward them.

"Duck!" Charlotte covered her head.

The cannon ball struck the rounded, armored roof. It rolled, zigzagged between the iron spikes and fell harmlessly into the water.

Jeffrey whooped. "We're indestructible! Let's go get'um!" He dug his oar deep into the water and pulled.

"Stick to the rhythm," Jeffrey's bench partner said. "You're just like the man who replaced Admiral Yi. He had no rules and no discipline for his forces to follow, and he lost most of the fleet. Have patience! Admiral

Yi's back in charge. Even when he had only twelve boats left, he was victorious. We'll win today too if," the seaman narrowed his eyes and glared at Jeffrey, "if we follow orders."

"Only twelve boats!" Jeffrey gulped and avoided Sabumnim's gaze.

On the deck above them, men rolled heavy balls into barrels of cannons shaped like crouching tigers.

"Fire!" Sounding like an echo, the order was repeated down the line of command to an officer on the upper deck. At his order, the soldiers lit the cannon fuses.

The turtle boat jolted as cannon balls shot toward the Japanese fleet of several hundred ships. Loud blasts from turtle boats in front and behind them vibrated the wooden benches.

"Fire 2! Fire 3!"

Soldiers jammed armloads of arrows down the mouths of small cannons. Flying sticks of fire shot out. "See?" Jeffrey's partner said. "Admiral Yi's invented arrows that ignite."

"Admiral Yi's boat is turning. Row port!" ordered the officer. The drummer increased the tempo.

The turtle boat took its place in the V formation, and Admiral Yi gave orders to bombard the trapped Japanese fleet.

The turtle boat pitched left, rolled into ocean swells, and threw Jeffrey into the aisle. Another seaman quickly replaced Jeffrey at the oar.

Unnoticed and freed from his duties, Jeffrey wasted no time moving from the shadowy lower deck through the smoke-filled upper deck to an open porthole. He gazed out into a rising swell of blue-green water.

The slow moving Japanese fleet bobbed in the middle of the V. Some of the fifty-foot Japanese ships were on fire and sinking. Their crews jumped overboard. Others continued on a course straight for Jeffrey's ship.

"Load cannons 5, 12, and 19." The echo rang through the levels.

Admiral Yi's ship, its oars plunging deep into the ocean, cut swiftly toward the lead vessel. Admiral Yi pulled close to the Japanese ship and fired his cannons. The mast on the Japanese ship broke in two and crashed to the deck below.

Jeffrey pressed his face against the porthole to get a better view. A flash of fire whipped past his nose. He pulled back as another flaming arrow skimmed the side of the boat. A shower of arrows pelted the roof, bounced off along with chunks of burning straw, and fizzled in the water.

Jeffrey spotted five Japanese ships closing quickly from the west.

"Boy, stoke the fire and throw in the saltpeter." A short, muscular seaman pushed Jeffrey toward a pile of dry wood and saltpeter lying beside a smoke generator. The man returned to his pile of yellow rocks and pounded them into smaller pieces. Motioning to Jeffrey to open the smoke generator's door, the man tossed the pieces into the fire. Jeffrey quickly followed with an armload of saltpeter.

"Phew!" Jeffrey held his nose. "It smells like rotten eggs!"

"Those yellow chunks are sulfur. Get used to it.

Mixed with saltpeter, it's one of our best defenses!" the man said. "It scares our enemy!"

Jeffrey noticed a pipe leading from the back of the generator and disappearing into the front of the boat and up the turtle head's neck. Grabbing another load of wood and saltpeter, Jeffrey threw them into the generator. The revolting smell from the yellow chunks of sulfur overpowered him, and he stumbled backwards.

"Move, boy!" A seaman loaded one of Admiral Yi's flame throwers.

Feeling sick to his stomach, Jeffrey leaned against the wall and lurched toward an open porthole. Surrounding turtle boats belched clouds of the foul-smelling smoke through the carved turtle heads mounted on the front of the ships. The Japanese sailors yelled in terror when they saw the fire breathing heads.

"Hard starboard." Yi's fleet turned. The smokey fog created by the turtle heads covered their change of course.

Muffled gun fire searched for a target in the fog.

"Guns!" Jeffrey yelled. "They have guns! Why aren't we using our guns?"

"Guns?" The captain put his hands on his hips. "What are you doing up here? Aren't you a rower?"

Jeffrey bowed and quickly backed down the stairs to the lower level. The boat rolled and flipped him into a wall. Jeffrey found his sea legs and peeked out another porthole.

The boat rose to the top of an enormous swell, and Jeffrey saw a Japanese ship close beside them.

The captain hoarsely shouted his order. "Coming

alongside. Cannons ready. Fire!"

Cannon balls blasted. Flaming arrows set fire to the enemy's sails and timber. The Koreans fired again and again.

The Japanese ship, equipped with only two cannons, was in trouble. Floating timbers and soldiers soon littered the water. The remainder of the Japanese fleet turned and fled, but the turtle boats, determined to prevent the Japanese from returning, relentlessly pursued them.

The turtle boats returned at last to the port. The men gathered on the shore, greeted one another and waited impatiently to hear Admiral Yi's victory speech.

"We should move on." Sabumnim reached for the ribbon floating on the water.

"No, please. I want to hear Admiral Yi's speech."

"Jeffrey . . ."

The men hushed, an eerie change from the noisy crowd just a few minutes before. A body, that of Admiral Yi, was carried ceremoniously from his boat.

His aide spoke. "Admiral Yi's last words were: 'Do not let the rest know I am dead, for it will spoil the fight.'" The men bowed in respect and sorrow.

"Admiral Yi's dead," Jeffrey said in disbelief. "I don't understand. He was in a boat that cannon balls and arrows couldn't damage."

"He was shot with a stray bullet. When people fight, there's always a price to pay. Sometimes the price is very high."

Jeffrey turned his back to the wharf. The threadbare ribbon snaked weightlessly in front of him, water dripping from its folds.

"Where to?" Charlotte asked.

"I don't care," Jeffrey mumbled. "I just want to leave here."

"Do you remember during the first day of class, we talked about the ribbon of time connecting the past, present, and future?"

Jeffrey nodded sadly.

"War, peace, greed, generosity, everything we do affects time and one another, even people and countries not directly involved. Korea, considered a 'little brother' by China, was still invaded time and time again by China as well as other countries. Finally, tired of fighting, Korea closed her borders to everyone."

Sabumnim stretched out his arm and the ribbon laid itself gently into his cupped hand. "Take the ribbon. We're traveling to a time known as the Hermit Kingdom."

# 19

# Hermit Kingdom Life

They plopped face down into an almost empty brass grain bin.

"Can't the ribbon ever find somewhere nice to put us?" Jeffrey spit a grain hull from his mouth.

Charlotte shook her head until all the hulls had flown from her ponytail.

An uneven tap, slide, tap, slide, tap came from behind a rice papered door. Charlotte slid it open an inch and peeked.

A woman sat cross-legged on a mat on one side of the sunken kitchen floor. A strip of cloth wound about a wooden roller. She hit the cloth with two sticks, ironing the material and giving it a gloss that made it look almost like silk.

Across from her, sat a three-year old girl wearing a bright yellow festival dress trimmed around the sleeves in red. Her dark hair was pulled back into a single, neat braid.

Outside the house, high pitched oboes screeched and drummers banged a procession melody. A cheering crowd followed the musicians to the town square.

The child hopped up. Her eyes appeared over-large in her gaunt face. The woman set aside the roller and sticks and draped a piece of cloth over her head. It shadowed her face and draped over her festive clothes, a soft blue, long flowing skirt and an embroidered, short blouse made of soft cotton. She reached a bony hand to the little girl.

They walked toward the celebration held in the village square. Soon the child tired and sat on the ground. The woman turned and sighed.

"Come, child. They will serve food after the dragons fight. Please try to walk. I can't carry you."

The little girl obediently crawled to her feet and shuffled after her mother to the town square.

Two huge, colorful, stuffed paper dragon heads topped long poles carried by men from different villages. One man from each team shinnied up a pole and sat behind a dragon head. Skinny fingers clung tightly to the back of each dragon's neck.

The two teams took their places. On command, they charged toward each other, crashing the dragon heads together. One rider slipped.

The crowd screamed, some cheerfully and others in despair.

"Hang on!" his teammates yelled. "You know what this means for our village and our crops."

The rider dragged himself back into position, hunger and strain showing on his face. The villagers ran again toward each other. Crash! This time he held on. The other man slipped.

"Get up! Get up!" his horrified teammates pleaded. For a third time, the villagers ran toward each other. The force of the jolt broke the first man's grip on the dragon, and he fell off the pole.

"We have the luck! Our harvest will be good next year!" The successful team cheered.

The disgraced rider picked himself up. "They'll just take your harvest from you in taxes," he said.

Most of his team dejectedly followed the victorious team to the feast. Women served the meal, giving everyone small portions.

The mother carried dishes over to an old man resting beneath the sparse shade of the forsythia shrubs. He put down his long pipe and picked up a brass spoon.

After the men and boys were served, the women and girls ate.

A group of men left and returned in full, festive regalia. Some wore masks. Everyone cleared a spot for them.

The musicians played and the men danced a comical mask dance-drama which made fun of priests and yangban. The audience forgot their hunger and troubles and laughed, enjoying the farce.

"Sabumnim," Jeffrey said. "These people are from two villages? There aren't many here and even so, there's hardly enough grain to feed them all winter."

"Effects, Jeffrey. They won their last war and yet. . . look around you."

Deserted houses, their thatched roofs worn and full of holes, lined the potted, muddy street. A broken tile on a deserted pagoda coasted noisily off the roof and landed on a heap of cracked tiles.

"Shouldn't they fix that stuff?"

"Many times in war the invaders take the educated and skilled people with them when they leave. Right now, there is no one who knows how to kiln fire tiles."

A young boy playing an oboe screeched another sour note.

"Or make music," Sabumnim said. "It's kind of like learning a new kick. It's difficult at first . . ."

"And then one day, after hours of practice, you can just do it." Jeffrey leapt into a perfect jumping front kick.

Charlotte tried to copy Jeffrey's moves. She skipped forward, stopped, jumped, and then threw out a low front kick. "Humph!"

"Don't worry. Someday you'll fly too," Jeffrey said.

"I wouldn't do Taek Kyun here."

The hoarse whisper surprised them, and they turned together. The boy with the oboe stood behind them. He wore a loose vest and pants tied at the waist.

"It no longer finds favor in the eyes of the king."

"If no one does it anymore, then how come you knew what we were doing?" Jeffrey found himself whispering just like the boy.

The boy studied them for a moment. He checked to make sure no one was within hearing distance before he spoke. "Meet me north of town near the Shamin totem poles." He lifted the oboe to his lips and blew another dreadful note before hurrying off to join the other musicians.

# 20

## Mountain Monastery

It didn't take long to find the colorful, wooden Shamin totem poles rising at the edge of a field of tall, unkempt grass and thick bushes. The poles guarded the entrance of an old, crooked path leading up the mountain. The ancient carved faces glared fiercely at the travelers. Wooden tongues curved out of huge, angry mouths.

"Are these supposed to scare off bad spirits too?" Charlotte asked.

"Yes. That's what the Shamin believed," Sabumnim said.

Charlotte touched the weathered tongue, and a loud snort came from behind the totem pole. Charlotte jumped.

"It's not the pole making noises, Charlotte." Jeffrey chuckled. "It's a boar."

Charlotte made a face at him.

Jeffrey pointed to the wild boar pawing the ground. At Jeffrey's quick movement, the boar snorted again and plunged away from them.

The dark-haired boy from town crouching in the long grass, gasped and jumped out of the boar's way.

The boy straightened the oboe slung by a strap over his shoulder. "Boars don't generally run away. We're lucky."

He cautiously approached Sabumnim, Charlotte, and Jeffrey. "This way. It's not too far."

He led them up the mountain path lined with bushes thick with berries. Magpies, in the middle of their supper, squawked and flew off. Long-tailed pheasants scurried under bushes looking for places to hide. Trees gradually replaced the low underbrush.

"Wolves and tigers live in this forest." The boy picked up a fallen branch. He slashed the air as if clearing an imaginary path. "I saw a tiger last week. Luckily, he wasn't hungry."

"Isn't there anything in here that won't eat us?" Charlotte looked carefully around her, peering into the deep spaces underneath dark bushes.

The boy thrust the branch at a bush and a rabbit ran out. "In our folk stories, clever rabbits outsmart even the mighty tiger. Some of our animals even speak wisely to us. But white tigers and blue dragons protect us and bring us good luck."

"Really?" Charlotte picked up a stick and struck another bush.

The nervous tension drained from the boy's shoulders. "Come. I will show you a dragon."

He raced ahead with Charlotte and Jeffrey close behind. The mountain path twisted back and forth. Dark green pines thrust their spiny needles amongst the brilliant red and yellow leaves of maple, oak and willow trees. A narrow, wooden footbridge crossed a wide stream. Clear water bubbled over smooth rocks and fish jumping for flies left ripples on the surface. Charlotte tiptoed on the slats and felt the bridge sway. She quickly adjusted her weight to move with it.

The mournful, low sound of a bell rumbled through the woods. Jeffrey saw sections of a walled monastery barely visible through colorful tree tops.

Bong! The low tones sounded again.

"It's a good day to visit. They only ring the bell for holidays, and today is the feast of the harvest moon."

A gaunt, bald monk opened the wooden gate and greeted them.

In the center of the courtyard stood a three tiered granite pagoda, built in memory of an earlier monk.

A one-story wooden temple stood almost a hundred feet behind it. Several monks walked prayerfully over a dirt path and past the stone lanterns. They removed their wooden shoes and entered the temple.

The outside eaves of the temple were painted in soft pastels; the blossoms on the temple doors were painted in soft blues, rusts and yellows.

Bong! Bong! Bong! A monk swung a gong and struck the seven-foot brass bell hanging in a large pavilion in the courtyard. The wooden pavilion stood on red columns over a granite floor. Red lotus blossoms were painted at the ends of the rafters which extended under the eaves of the gray tiled roofs.

The boy stepped up to the intricately painted bell.

"There's the dragon. Look! Up there. It's part of the handle which attaches the bell to the beam." The boy's head tilted so far backwards, Jeffrey thought he'd fall over.

Charlotte followed the boy's gaze to the ornamental hook shaped like a dragon. She walked closer.

"Did you see this? Fairies are dancing on the sides of the bell." Charlotte lightly ran her fingers across the raised metal figures.

The boy bowed to the monk. "Do you know where Master Sung is?"

"You will find him in the work room." The monk replaced the gong.

The boy led the way to a building nestled next to a pond. They walked across a granite bridge and entered an enormous room. A few monks sat at tables in an area once filled with hundreds of craftsmen.

An elderly monk sat cross-legged on the floor and played an oboe. Rich, full tones echoed throughout the empty work room. His fingers moved confidently over the keys, playing a slow, haunting melody.

Another monk wove baskets out of bamboo. Using his mouth and hands, he split the reeds into thin halves. With flying fingers, he built a strong base for the circular basket and interwove the remaining strips into its sides.

The boy led Sabumnim, Jeffrey, and Charlotte to a monk painting quietly in a corner.

Master Sung sat hunched over a wooden chest. His fingers gently pressed a fine-bristled brush. Strokes of white paint delicately danced across a red background, forming the face of a white tiger. Master Sung studied his feathery strokes, put down his brush and wiped his hands. Not until then did he greet his visitors.

"Master Sung." The boy bowed. "I have friends I would like you to meet. They are interested in Taek Kyun."

Master Sung greeted Sabumnim and dismissed the boy. Jeffrey watched, curious as to what the boy would do now. The boy walked over and bowed to the musician, removed the oboe from his shoulder strap and sat cross-legged in front of the monk. He brought the oboe to his lips and screeched a few notes. The monk shook his head and spoke. Again the boy blew. This time, the note was solid.

"Yes!" Jeffrey clenched his fist.

"You are interested in Taek Kyun?" Master Sung asked.

Charlotte nudged Jeffrey, and he turned back. "Yes. But he said it's not popular anymore."

"Knowledge and study of Confucian writings are encouraged by the Yi dynasty. The government frowns on the study of the martial arts," said Master Sung. "But it still lives on in places like ours in the mountains or is taught in the dark of night in the cities. People have many reasons to learn Taek Kyun, including protection."

Master Sung walked to the center of the room and asked Jeffrey and Charlotte to stand in front of him.

The boy who had been playing beautiful notes suddenly hit another sour one.

Jeffrey winced. "I thought he finally had it."

"Show me a reverse turning kick."

Jeffrey and Charlotte stepped into fighting stances. Charlotte checked the placement of her hands and feet to make sure they were correct. She turned around, but slowly.

Meanwhile, Jeffrey whipped around. But his head moved more slowly than his body, and he lost his balance.

Master Sung nodded. "Just because you can do something once or even a few times, doesn't mean it will always be right. Perfection requires practice and concentration." He circled around them. "Now defend against an attack from the side."

Charlotte lifted her leg, bent it at the knee and kicked to the side. Her leg fell straight to the floor.

"Try again. Remember to pull your knee back into the chamber when you are finished kicking."

Sabumnim came closer and held out his hand as a target. Charlotte practiced chambering her side kick. Master Sung nodded in approval and turned to Jeffrey.

"Show me an offensive attack."

Jeffrey mechanically threw a back fist. The old monk stepped in, blocked Jeffrey's fist and planted a punch to Jeffrey's ribs.

Jeffrey's eyes widened in surprise.

"Look first. You must see your imaginary opponent. It may mean the difference between saving your life or losing it."

The children and Master Sung bowed to each other.

"Fine new students." Master Sung and Sabumnim exchanged a knowing look and bowed. "You've already met my new student. He has many undeveloped talents, and he will need them all. I have chosen him to take my place when I am gone."

The ribbon, worn yet flecked with spots of midnight blue glitter, floated down between the two groups.

"Have a good journey, travelers," Master Sung said.

# 21

## Marketplace

Chickens squawked and feathers flew as the mist cleared. The travelers stood in the middle of a noisy, narrow marketplace. People hurried between shopsinto the crowded street. Merchants carried goods on their backs, and some set up shop on mats laid out on the dusty ground. Children played in the street and chased the chickens.

A chicken peddler raced frantically after his birds. The woven bamboo box on his back bounced with each leap. He captured one chicken by its brown tail feathers. It squawked louder and turned to peck the peddler, who stuffed the chicken, head first, into the box.

A grandfather carried his grandson strapped to his back. The baby peered curiously at the sights and sounds, chuckling at the peddler and his chickens.

Once the first chicken was safe, the peddler sneaked up on the other who was busily scratching dirt and pecking at bugs in the street. The peddler quickly wrapped his fingers around the hen's neck and dropped her into the carry-all. The bird's claws gripped the upper

edge of the carry-all, and she pecked at the peddler's
hat brim.

The peddler found a shop selling fresh fruit.

"I want some oranges." The peddler slid his shoulders out of the cords tied to the carry-all and set it on
the table. The hens cackled, and small tufts of black,
white and brown feathers flew out and landed on the
merchant's table.

The merchant sniffed. "Don't you have money?"

"Money? Chickens were always good before."

"Times have changed. I bought these oranges from a farmer on the southern islands. I don't barter. I only accept paper money or brass coins for the goods I sell." The merchant pushed the carry-all toward the peddler, and it wobbled on the edge of the table.

The peddler rescued the carry-all and slid his arms through the cords.

"You must be one of those new, middle-man merchants I've heard about."

"And a new yangban, too." The man smirked. "Since we no longer have to know how to write Chinese or be born in the upper class to be a yangban, I bought the title. I can get a government job now."

The peddler scratched his chin. He walked down the alley toward Sabumnim. "Chickens for sale! Fat chickens for sale! Paper money or coins only!"

"Boy, does he learn fast," Jeffrey said to Sabumnim as the three forced their way through the excited crowd.

An old man, his gray topknot covered by a tall, horsehair hat, sold wooden shoes on a mat by the side of the road. A woman with an enormous umbrella-shaped bamboo hat covering her face selected a pair.

Behind the shoe seller flowed a stream of water in a ditch. Foot bridges crossed the ditch to thatched buildings on the other side. Several people sat at the bottom of the ditch washing their hands in the water.

A water carrier loosened one of the cords holding up a wooden backpack he bore on his back. A long pole was tied to the top of the back and braced against his lower back. Nine-inch iron hooks hung from both ends of the pole and linked through brackets on top of two wooden pails. He slid the cords off his shoulders, unhooked the pails and filled them with water from the stream. He hooked them to the pole. Sliding the cords over his shoulders, he bent his knees and stood. The two pails rocked gently with the motion.

A foul stench filled the air. Jeffrey sniffed, wrinkling his nose and looking questioningly at Sabumnim.

"That's where they wash. It also drains away their garbage and waste. It's not very clean. They have a lot of trouble with smallpox and other diseases."

A pock-marked dealer looking for a place to sell his goods towed an ox carrying firewood. The ox balked, lowered his head and smelled the wooden shoes laid out on a mat. He pushed them with his nose, tipping some over into the dirt. The dealer pulled and tugged, finally moving the ox.

A young vendor, his horsehair hat tied tightly under his chin, strolled through the crowd. A farmer approached him and bargained for one of the tall hats stacked on an A-frame rack on the vendor's back.

"Make way. Make way." Charlotte heard a rattling of cast iron wheels. A well-dressed man rode in a rickshaw pulled by a young man. The rider ignored much of what went on around him, fanning himself with a painted mulberry paper fan. The rickshaw driver glanced often to the right and left. The right wheel rolled over a wooden shoe. Shouting unintelligibly, the shoe seller threw a rock at the departing rickshaw.

Charlotte walked to the raised back door of a shop. She paused. A woman dropped three-inch cocoons into steaming hot water. Charlotte entered through the back door and peered into the pot. The hot water melted the natural glue holding the cocoons together. Long fibers separated and swam on top of the water. The woman picked up a loose end and wound the thin threads around a square wooden frame. Another woman took the frame and dipped it into a kettle of warm water.

"What are you doing?"

"We're making threads from the silk worm cocoon. We'll dye and weave them into fine silk fabric."

Voices erupted from the front of the shop. Charlotte slid open the mulberry paper door and stuck her head into the next room. A merchant removed a pale blue robe and draped it over the arms of a finely dressed young nobleman. The young nobleman paid the merchant.

"Just like that robe?" Charlotte asked.

The woman nodded and dropped more cocoons into the water.

Jeffrey crossed the narrow alley to a thatched hut and saw a potter sitting at a kickwheel in the dark room. The potter coiled a thin string of clay around a flat, clay disk centered on the wheel. He guided the formation of the pot with a round, wooden anvil and a flat, fan-shaped, wooden paddle. As he worked, he changed the direction and speed of the kickwheel. When he finished, the man formed a thick rim around the upper edges by turning the lip under. He spread a mixture of clay, ashes, and manganese oxide on the pot, picked up a sharp tool and etched a lotus flower design.

"Now it's ready for the kiln." The man placed the pot to one side.

A mustached man poked his head into the hut and removed the long pipe from his mouth. Instead of a hat, he wore a piece of dark cloth tied around his forehead. "Have any more pots for me to sell?" The potter peddler carried at least eight middle-sized, brown glazed pots and twenty smaller sized bowls on an A-frame on his back.

"Sabumnim." Jeffrey turned away. "These are a lot plainer than the ones we saw in the shop in the city during Shilla's time."

"They were making fine porcelain for royalty. This man is making glazed kimchee pots. He's thought to have one of the lowest jobs around," Sabumnim said. "It's believed some of the first Christians in Korea avoided persecution by taking up this trade. Some Catholics survived by hiding temporarily in large kimchee pots. The government didn't approve of outside religions."

Animal squeals pierced the market's bedlam. They watched a man wrestle with a brown pig. "I paid for you. You're mine!" The pig kicked, but the man latched onto its back hoof and lifted it up.

"Testing for government jobs today. Open to anyone who can pay, even bondsmen," a crier announced.

"What's a bondsman?" Charlotte asked.

"Sort of like a slave," Jeffrey said.

A jewelry merchant ordered the young man working with him to take over his shop. The merchant raided the money bag and left, joining others on their way to the testing site.

A farmer, selling wares from an A-frame, slipped it off his back, entered the testing area and sat at a low table.

"They must be giving the test in Hangul," Jeffrey said.

The sunlight suddenly dimmed. Jeffrey, Charlotte, and Sabumnim looked up. Pale and sheer, the ribbon drifted down on them and whisked them forward.

# 22

# The Assassination

The blue mist cleared, but they were still surrounded by gray smoke that was gradually swept away. A loud whistle blasted, and Jeffrey stared into the face of a giant steam engine. Its whistle blared at them again.

Feeling a metal rail digging into his foot, Jeffrey looked down at a railroad track.

"Here, Charlotte," Jeffrey cupped his hands. "That ribbon is going to kill us one of these days."

Charlotte balanced on her hands and boosted herself onto the platform next to Sabumnim. Jeffrey gripped the edge and pulled himself up.

Bursting coal cars, one attached to the other, sat on the track until they blurred in the distance into one long dark line.

Chinese characters covered the sides of the train cars and station.

"I thought Koreans were using the Hangul language now," Jeffrey said.

"They do. But we're in China at the Harbin Railroad station in Manchuria, right on the border of Korea. The

Japanese transport many Korean goods and supplies through this station."

"The people are going to be warm this winter." Jeffrey walked down the platform past the coal cars toward a crowd gathering on the far end.

"Not our people," an angry young man said. "Our rice is feeding people in other countries. Our coal heats others' homes, while we starve and freeze."

"One day we'll have our freedom," his companion said.

The coal train blew its whistle and chugged out of the station. Another train sounded its arrival. The crowd pushed to get closer to the new train. The mumbling increased.

"What's happening?" Jeffrey asked.

"Hirobumi Ito is coming here to meet with the Russian representative."

"Who's he?" Charlotte asked.

"Hirobumi Ito was a powerful Japanese statesman. He even studied in England. In 1905, he was appointed the first Japanese Governor General of Korea. He caused Korean officials to sign a secret treaty giving the Japanese the right to occupy Korea," Sabumnim said. "The Korean people found out and organized guerrilla fighting forces which they located in Manchuria and in Siberia. By 1909, Japan turned over part of Korea to the Chinese so the Japanese could mine the rich mineral fields of Manchuria."

"They just gave part of Korea to another country?" Jeffrey asked.

"Yes. And the Russians are concerned about Japan's interest in their country, since Manchuria borders Siberia. So they are meeting Hirobumi Ito here today to talk about it."

The sleek, polished political train pulled to a stop. The whistle blew twice.

A man with white hair, mustache and beard stepped off the train. He lifted his black bowler hat to the uniformed Russians waiting to meet him. The crowd closed in.

"We had better move on. It's 1909." Sabumnim hustled them toward the road leading away from the station.

Sharp, staccato sounds rang out. Sabumnim glanced over his shoulder. People scrambled to get away from the soldiers and the station. Sabumnim increased their pace.

"What happened?" Jeffrey strained to see.

"Hirobumi Ito was assassinated by An Joong Gun, a young teacher turned guerilla leader. Despite raids like these, Japan annexed Korea and made it part of Japan in 1910."

"What happened to Mr. An?" Jeffrey asked.

"He was imprisoned at Lui-Shung prison and executed five months later."

"Why did the ribbon bring us here?" Charlotte asked.

"Anything that was Korean was banned after the annexation. Their traditional topknots, their customs, even their written language was forbidden. The Japanese destroyed most of Korea's historical records. Schools taught only in Japanese so many children suddenly could not read or write because the language was changed. People couldn't get jobs and became a class of slave workers. They weren't educated for anything.

"The ribbon brought us here because from this time on, Taek Kyun was outlawed by the Japanese. It was practiced only in secret by a few fathers and sons. Many martial artists left the country all together."

"I've had enough of wars and guns," Charlotte said. Jeffrey watched his sister nervously twisting her ponytail. "Come on, Charlotte. I'll give you a ride." Jeffrey bent over and Charlotte climbed on his back, piggy-back style. Taking big steps, he galloped along the dirt road, bouncing Charlotte.

"Wait, Jeffrey," Sabumnim shouted. "You don't want to get ahead in time."

"What?" Jeffrey spun around to face Sabumnim and continued to jog backwards.

Sabumnim gestured at the ribbon lying silently on the road. Jeffrey had crossed the 1910 marker. The wind gusted, and the ribbon billowed violently. A loud r-r-r-r-rip split the air behind Jeffrey and Charlotte. Jeffrey whipped around toward the noise. The ribbon's fabric, tossed in the sudden wind, began to shred in two long strips. The mutilated edges tore faster and faster toward them.

"Sabumnim!" Jeffrey tried to jump out of the way, but the wider strip wrapped around Charlotte's feet and separated them from Sabumnim.

Sabumnim leapt for them but a sliver of ribbon detached and floated into the mist taking Sabumnim with it.

The ribbon's tattered fabric wrapped around Charlotte and Jeffrey and misted forward into time.

# 23

## Japanese Garden

In a parachute of fabric, the ribbon cradled them to the ground. Jeffrey rolled from its bellows and pulled Charlotte out. Their part of the ribbon, once again satiny and heavenly blue, whisked itself high over their heads and disappeared.

"Oh no, Jeffrey! We've lost Sabumnim!"

"We got the big part of the ribbon, so naturally, we just got here first." Jeffrey folded his arms to hide his shaking hands.

"Where's here?"

They explored the unusual garden in which they had landed. Short trees and shrubs were trimmed and wired into twisting shapes. Many grew in pots of various sizes. Wavy lines looking like ripples on a pond were raked into the white sand covering the ground at the base of the trees and bushes.

"Those are bonsai trees. This must be Japan," Jeffrey said.

"KIAI." A karate battle yell came from beyond the cherry trees.

Jeffrey and Charlotte spread branches of fragrant, pink cherry blossoms.

Two men moved in unison on the white sand. Their arms whipped into left knife hand strikes. They lifted their right legs high, rotated and snapped their bent legs to full length.

"At least we're in modern times. Their hair is short, like ours," Jeffrey whispered.

Movements were performed singly or in combinations. They moved into a strike, their bodies relaxed and fluid until the moment of impact. Then, all their power focused on one imaginary spot before turning fluid again.

Their intense faces reflected their concentration. They ended with a middle punch and returned to a ready stance. All intensity gone, they bowed to each other.

One entered a school building at the end of the garden.

The other young man stretched his athletic body and did cooling down exercises.

"You can come out now," he said.

Jeffrey released the branches. They snapped shut, showering the ground with cherry blossoms.

"How did you know we were here?" Jeffrey shielded Charlotte behind him.

"You must always be aware of your surroundings."

"That's what Sabumnim said."

"And you whisper loudly!"

Charlotte stepped from behind Jeffrey, folded her arms and glared at Jeffrey. "We're lost."

"No, we're not. We're separated." Jeffrey returned Charlotte's glare.

"I know how it is to be alone in a new place. I am from Korea myself. You may stay here until your Sabumnim comes for you." The man bowed to them. "I must practice calligraphy now. If you'd like, you can practice too."

They sat outside under cherry trees at low tables covered with clean sheets of paper, brushes, and containers of ink. Dipping his brush, the young man stroked a short horizontal line over a longer one with a circle touching it. Under that he brushed an upside down T. Next to that column he painted a vertical line intersected just below midpoint by a line extending to the right. The next character looked like the letter 2 over a circle. He finished up with a vertical line, again intersected with a short slash to the right.

"This is the Hangul character for Hwarang. Now you try."

Charlotte brushed a curving line on her white paper. Pale pink cherry blossoms drifted onto the wet, jet black ink. She blew at the petals, but that only fluttered their edges and sank their centers deeper into the ink. Charlotte sighed and plucked the petals off, one-by-one.

Jeffrey eagerly inked his brush and yanked it from the ink well. Splotches of ink spilled all over his paper.

The young man grinned. "Like most arts, it takes practice and patience. Focus on one move at a time."

Noisy chatter erupted from the doorway of the school building.

"I must leave you for awhile. If anyone asks for me, you haven't seen me." He joined his friends.

"Why haven't we seen him?" Charlotte asked.

They went to the school's door and saw the young men enter an empty classroom.

"Remember Sabumnim saying that many Koreans fought for independence from Japan? Some must have fought even while living in Japan." Jeffrey stepped inside.

Charlotte wandered into an open, empty office. On a desk, two foot-long sticks connected with a piece of rope held down a neat stack of papers. She picked up one end and let it dangle full length. She spun the other half in wide swishing circles, blowing the papers off the desk onto the floor.

Jeffrey peeked in. "Whoa! Careful! That's a *sang jul gon.*" He gathered the papers and returned them neatly to the desk.

Charlotte switched hands and twirled with her left. "Look, Jeffrey." She walked closer. The swirling end glanced off Jeffrey's arm.

He blocked and took the sang jul gon away from Charlotte. "This is a weapon. It can hurt!"

"Sorry. Why put two sticks together for a weapon?"

"In Okinawa, it used to be a horse bit." Jeffrey twirled it around and caught one end under his arm.

"Since farmers were not allowed to carry weapons, they used whatever was handy for protection." Jeffrey handed the sang jul gon to Charlotte. "Here, try it again. But stand over there!"

Charlotte hesitantly whipped the sang jul gon around, slowly gaining control.

"Now after you twirl it, flip it and catch the other end under your arm." Jeffrey stepped back.

Charlotte twirled, flipped, and caught it. She giggled. "I have to show this to our new friend." She clutched the two ends and ran out the door.

"Jeffrey!"

The ribbon hung near the ceiling. Bit by bit, it deliberately unrolled its satiny folds until it draped gracefully to the floor and blocked the hall.

"I will never quit until Korea's free." The young man's voice echoed from the other side of the ribbon.

"Maybe Sabumnim's with him."

"Let's look. Hang on, just in case." Jeffrey handed her the end of his dobok.

Charlotte dropped the sang jul gon on the floor.

Jeffrey nudged the ribbon aside and walked through the mist.

# 24

# In Prison

Jeffrey and Charlotte stepped into a dark, damp underground walkway. Hands gripped iron bars cemented into cell doors.

"We're in jail," Charlotte said. "Sabumnim's never going to find us here."

They tiptoed down the hall of caged men. Charlotte saw an open cell door and tightened her grip on Jeffrey.

"KIAI!" A man cried.

Jeffrey and Charlotte stared. Two young prisoners sparred with prison guards. The men shuffled around the narrow cell, grunting when a punch landed.

One of the prisoners noticed the travelers and abruptly stopped punching. The guard glanced curiously over his shoulder and straightened when he saw the children.

"What are you doing here?" He charged through the open door.

Jeffrey and Charlotte gasped. Jeffrey looked around for an escape route. The ribbon hung at the far end of the hall.

"Run, Charlotte!" He raced for the ribbon.

Charlotte's short legs tried to keep up with him.

"Did you see who the prisoner was?" Jeffrey huffed. "That was our friend from the garden. He and his friends must have tried to fight the Japanese."

Ahead of them, the ribbon rested on the floor. Puffing up with air, it rose and hovered about a foot off the floor. Its smooth edges rippled, inviting them to sit.

Charlotte's heart pounded. The guard's short, rasping breath echoed right behind her. She could feel his fingertips searching for a grip on her uniform. Charlotte dropped and crouched into a ball. Unable to stop in time, the guard tripped and flew over her, crashing into the wall.

"Way to go, Charlotte!"

She picked herself up, and they leapt onto the rolling surface. The ribbon flew from the dingy jail and into the blue mist of time.

# 25
# World War II

Deep in the mist, a propeller engine roared. The ribbon pitched sharply to the right. Jeffrey poked out his head.

A World War II fighter swooped out of the mist and headed straight for Jeffrey. He ducked. The force of the fighter twisted the ribbon around and around, thrusting Jeffrey inside. He spied the blue mist through a tiny gap in the fabric. He pressed his eye to the hole and watched. A second plane chased the first. A burst of machine gun fire ripped the mist before both planes disappeared.

"Are we going to stop at another war?" Charlotte said.

"We just passed World War II."

The ribbon dipped. The mist thickened and swirled around them. The ribbon twirled once then unfolded into a silky, flying carpet.

They broke through the mist and the triangular Korean peninsula appeared. The year 1948 formed on the shimmering folds of the blue ribbon just   before it descended.

They skimmed the top of a Korean military base. Men gassed planes for the next training class and rolled them out to the runways.

Passing a recreational hall, the ribbon dipped to window height. They caught sight of a martial arts class inside.

"I see some American soldiers in there with the Korean soldiers," Jeffrey said.

The ribbon turned a deeper shade of blue, picked up speed and a year flashed by.

# 26
# Coming Home?

When the mist cleared, the familiar shape of the United States appeared.

"We're home!" Jeffrey shouted.

The ribbon gravitated toward an American army base. A huge welcome banner hung outside a brick gymnasium. The ribbon picked up speed and hurled toward the banner. The children screamed and covered their eyes. They felt a slight tug on their bodies as they passed through the wall.

A loud round of applause and cheers rose. Jeffrey spread his fingers and peeked. They circled in the rafters high above a gym floor and a crowd of cheering soldiers watching a demonstration.

"The martial arts have come to the U.S.," Jeffrey said.

A small man bowed to the crowd. Two men faced him, bowed and attacked. The lone man instantly responded with a twin jumping front snap kick, each foot directed at one of the men.

"There's a new one for you, Jeffrey!"

Again the ribbon sped up. This time, Jeffrey and Charlotte watched as they were sucked through the wall. Tiny brown, yellow and red molecules glimmered and swooshed by the travelers. The molecules turned five shades of blue and misted.

# 27
# The Korean War

Deep inside the misty fog, Jeffrey and Charlotte felt a wild wind resisting the ribbon's descent and shoving them upwards. They gripped the ribbon. It bucked twice and burst through a hole in the mist.

They scanned the green hills and snow covered mountains of the Korean peninsula. The year 1952 appeared in bold numbers.

The ribbon sailed above planes dropping bombs, burning buildings and black clouds of smoke.

It flew through the Korean War directly to the Korean President's headquarters.

Jeffrey and Charlotte laid flat on the ribbon and surveyed the gathering of martial arts masters performing their styles for the President.

Some of the masters performed sweeping hand movements and kicks while others demonstrated flying kicks and precision punches. One martial artist broke a tall stack of roof tiles with a single blow.

The President, pleased with the demonstration, turned and spoke to his military advisor.

The ribbon swooped upwards and transported them to an office at military headquarters.

Jeffrey and Charlotte lowered their heads over the flapping edge of the ribbon.

"We want you to use your skills as spies," an officer said.

Several martial artist masters listened intently to instructions and bowed in agreement.

The ribbon's edges curled, tumbling Jeffrey and Charlotte into the center. The ribbon's fibers grew stronger and the blue mist pulsated around them.

When the mist cleared, pineapples, bananas, and figs covered the ribbon. They rode on a gentle tropical breeze and dipped toward an island off the southern coast of Korea. Jeffrey peeled a banana and handed an orange to Charlotte.

They cruised past a flag pole of a Korean army base. Hundreds of men worked out in small groups. One group practiced turning kicks and flying side kicks while another section worked on blocking techniques.

Charlotte watched a man protect himself by taking two attackers to the ground. He shouted a command to others in his section who broke into groups of three. Each man practiced the take-downs.

Jeffrey pointed to a section with ten straight lines of men. At the leader's command, they moved forward doing combination hand and foot techniques. Another group to their right practiced a form.

Jeffrey's eyes darted excitedly from one group to another. "I bet they're combining some of the different martial arts techniques down there!"

# 28

# Past and Present United

The ribbon rose sharply and took Jeffrey and Charlotte higher than they had ever flown before. The strong and sturdy ribbon swooped around a curve. Visions of their travels snagged on the ribbon's fabric and became real. Generals, farmers, monks, Mongols, bandits, and kings rode the ribbon, some hanging from the ribbon's edges.

The ribbon lurched into a downward spiral, tunneling everyone inside. The fabric formed roller coaster loops. Jeffrey and Charlotte slid right-side up and upside-down through the thinning mist until the ribbon widened and leveled off in a large room. Jeffrey and Charlotte were alone on the ribbon.

Below them, officials finished their discussion. The ribbon was marked 1955.

The ribbon deflated and set them among the spectators watching the proceedings.

A solemn official rustled his papers, cleared his throat and announced their decision to follow General Choi's suggestion and name the Korean martial art,

Taekwondo. "We selected the name Taekwondo because it means the art of hand and foot fighting and it sounds like Taek Kyun, Korea's ancient martial art."

Charlotte saw Sabumnim in the crowd. "Sabumnim!" She scrambled from the ribbon.

Sabumnim waved and worked his way through the spectators. He heaved a sigh of relief and smiled broadly.

"You had doubts?" Jeffrey rose gracefully to his feet.

"I choose my travelers carefully. But you're the first set I've ever been separated from." He smiled wryly. "I think the ribbon's developed an attitude."

The ribbon flowed gently around their feet. Faces and events from the past appeared again. This time, they became colorful etchings woven permanently within the threads of the fabric.

Won Hyo carried his lute and was surrounded by large groups of people. Admiral Yi stood tall again, leading his men into battle, and the brave Hwarangdo youth studied and trained in their camps.

Finally, Sabumnim's face appeared. Within seconds, the faint images of a little girl with a ponytail on top of her head and a tall, gangly boy rose on the fabric.

"I think I understand now how the ribbon of history connects the past and its people to the present," Jeffrey said.

Charlotte smiled, rubbed her graying belt, and nodded. "It's time to make our own history."

The three joined hands. A glorious blue mist rose and the radiant ribbon gathered them into its silky folds. . .

# Glossary

**Ap chagi**      Front kick

**Baekje**        (baek•jae) One of the four kingdoms, located in the southwestern part of the peninsula. Legend states it was founded in 18 B.C.

**Chagi**         (cha•gi) Kick

**Charyut**       (cha•ri•ut) Attention stance

**Choson**        The name of the kingdom on the Korean peninsula during the Yi dynasty which was 1392 -1910 A.D.

**Chumoni**       A bag worn by men and women around their necks to carry their personal belongings.

**Confucian**     The system of ethics, education, and statesmanship taught by Confucius and his disciples.

**Dangun**        Legendary founder of Korea in 2333 B.C. The legend of his mystical birth served as a source of strength and national pride especially during the Shilla, Koryo and Yi dynasties.

**Dobok**         (to•bok) Uniform worn for Taekwondo practice.

**Dojang**        (to•chang) Taekwondo school or training place.

**Golden Age**    Time of peace during the Shilla dynasty, 688 to 935 A.D.

**Hangul**        The Korean alphabet consisting of 24 characters.

**Hanyang**       Capitol established by Yi Song-gye for the Choson dynasty. Later known as Seoul.

**Hwarangdo**     (hoa•rang•do) Youth warrior group during the Shilla period which helped unify the four kingdoms.

**Joochoom sogi**  (ju•chum so•gi)  Horse riding stance

**Kaya**  One of the four ancient kingdoms, located in the south-central part of the peninsula. Legend states it was founded in 42 A.D. Little known, it was conquered by the Shilla kingdom by 562 A.D.

**Kihap**  A loud cry which expels air, helps focus power, and startles the opponent.

**Kimchee**  Spicy, pickled vegetables

**Kobukson**  Turtle boat

**Koguryo**  (ko•kur•yo)  One of the four kingdoms located in the northern part of the peninsula. Legend states it was founded in 37 B.C.

**Koryo dynasty**  The kingdom (918 A.D.-1392 A.D.) following the downfall of Shilla. It was followed by the Yi dynasty.

**Kyongju**  The capital of the Shilla kingdom.

**Kyungye**  (kyung•yae)  Bow

**Naeryu chagi**  Axe kick

**Ondol**  Traditional heated floor found in Korean homes.

**Pusan**  Port city located in Shilla, on the southeast coast.

**Sabum**  Instructor

**Sabumnim**  Title used to address one's instructor, honorific form of sabum.

**Sang Jul Gon**  Two hardwood sticks connected by rope or chains. The weapon, also called nunchaku, originated in Okinawa.

| | |
|---|---|
| **Shijak** | (shi•ch'ak) Begin |
| **Shilla** | One of the four ancient kingdoms, located in the southeastern part of thep eninsula. Legend states it was founded in 57 B.C. |
| **Shilla dynasty** | Shilla unified the four kingdoms by 688 A.D. and ruled until 935 A.D. when it was taken over by the Koryo dynasty . |
| **Sogi** | Stance |
| **Subak** | Ancient form of martial arts which came from China and was practiced in      the north. |
| **Taejo** | (t'ae•jo) Founding father of Choson. |
| **Taek Kyun** | (t'aek•kyon) Ancient form of martial arts practiced by Hwarangdo. |
| **Taekwondo** | (t'ae•koan•do) Korean martial art. |
| **Wuryo chagi** | Sweep kick |
| **Yangban** | Aristocrats of the Yi dynasty. |
| **Yi dynasty** | It followed the Koryo dynasty and ruled until Japanese takeover in 1910. |
| **Yut** | Game pieces which are flat on one side and rounded on the other side. |
| **Yut Nori** | Traditional Korean game played with yut. |

The terminology used in *A Part of the Ribbon* is the current standard usage in Korea today. However, some schools may use different words to refer to the same movement. Each term was chosen because it is the most common word used, but not necessarily the only correct word to use. Students are encouraged to follow the customs of their dojang.

# Bibliography

A HANDBOOK OF KOREA, Korean Overseas Information Service Ministry of Culture and Information, Seoul, Korea, 1979

A HISTORY OF KOREA, William E. Henthorn, The Free Press, A Division of The Macmillan Company, 1971

A HISTORY OF KOREA, by Takashi Hatada, American Bibliographical Center, Clio Press, 1969

A NEW HISTORY OF KOREA, By Ki-baik Lee, Harvard University Press, Cambridge, Massachusetts, London, England,1984

AN INSIDERS GUIDE TO KOREA, by Peter Popham, Hunter Publishing Inc., Edison, New Jersey, 1987

CHINA Its History and Culture, by W. Scott Morton, McGraw-Hill Inc., 1980

COMPREHENSIVE ASIA FIGHTING ARTS, By Donn F. Draeger Robert W. Smith, Kodansha International, Tokyo, New York, London 1980.

CUSTOMS AND MANNERS IN KOREA, edited by International Cultural Foundation, The Si-sa-yong-o-sa Publishers, Inc., Korea

FIRST ENCOUNTERS, KOREA 1880-1910, Edited by Peter A. Underwood, Samuel H. Moffett & Norman R. Sibley, published by Dragon' Eye Graphics, Seoul,Korea, 1982

HANDBOOK OF KOREA, by Chae Kyung Oh, Pageant Press, Inc. New York, 1958

KOREA AN INTRODUCTION, James Hoare and Susan Pares, Kegan Paul International Limited, London, 1988

KOREA BEYOND THE HILLS, BY H. Edward Kim, Eulyoo Publishing Company, LTD., 1985

KOREA JOURNAL, Vol. 13, No. 12 December 1973

KOREA OLD AND NEW A HISTORY, Ilchokak, Publishers for the Korea Institute, Harvard University, Seoul, Korea, 1990

KOREAN CULTURE, Vol. 3, No. 4 December 1982

KOREAN CULTURE, Vol. 4, No. 1 March 1983

KOREAN CULTURE, Vol. 4, No. 3 September 1983

KOREAN CULTURE, Vol. 6, No. 2 June 1985

KOREAN CULTURE, Vol. 7, No. 3 September 1986

KOREAN CULTURE, Vol. 8, No. 1 March 1987

KOREAN CULTURE, Vol. 8, No. 2 Summer 1987

KOREAN CULTURE, Vol. 8, No. 3 Fall 1987

KOREAN CULTURE, Vol. 10, No. 1 Spring 1989

KOREAN CULTURE, Vol. 10, No. 2 Summer 1989

KOREAN CULTURE, Vol. 10, No. 3 Fall 1989

KOREAN DANCE, THEATER & CINEMA, edited by the Korean National Commission for UNESCO, The si-sa-yong-o-sa Publishers, Inc., Korea; Pace International Research, Inc., U.S.A., 1983
KOREAN WOMEN View From the Inner Room, edited by Laurel Kendall and Mark Peterson, East Rock Press, Inc., New Haven, Connecticut 1983

KOREANA, Korean Art & Culture, Vol. 7, No. 3 Autumn 1993

KOREANA, Korean Art & Culture, Vol. 7, No. 4 Winter 1993

KOREANA, Korean Art & Culture, Vol. 8, No. 3 Autumn 1994

KOREA'S CULTURAL ROOTS, by Dr. Jon Carter Covell, third edition, Moth House Publications, Salt Lake City; Hollym Corporation: Korea, 1981

KOREA'S HERITAGE A Regional and Social Geography, by Shannon McCune, Charles E. Tuttle Company, Rutland, Vermont, 1956

NAVAL SURGEON IN YI KOREA, The Journal of George W. Woods, edited by Fred C. Bohm and Robert R. Swartout, Jr., Institute of East Asian Studies, 1984

NORTH AND SOUTH KOREA, by Gene and Clare Gurney, Franklin Watts, Inc., New York, 1973

SEOUL CITY GUIDE, Korea National Tourism Corporation

TAE KWON DO, SECRETS OF KOREAN KARATE, by Sihak Henry Cho, Charles Tuttle Company; Rutland, Vermont & Tokyo, Japan 1993.

TAE KWON DO TIMES, Martial Arts, Fitness, and Health, Vol. 15 No. 3, December 1994, "Keep It Korean" by Thomas K. Waters.

THE HISTORY OF KOREA, by Woo-keun Han, Eul-Yoo Publishing Co., Ltd, 1970, paperback edition published by The University Press of Hawaii 1974.

THE HISTORY OF TAE-KWON DO PATTERNS, by Richard L. Mitchell, Lilley Gulch TKD, 1987

THE KOREANS AND THEIR CULTURE, C. Osgood, U-M-I Out of Print Books on Demand, 1988

THE PREHISTORY OF KOREA, by Jeong-Hak Kim, The University Press of Hawaii, Honolulu, 1978 (translation copyright)

THROUGH GATES OF SEOUL, By Edward B. Adams, Vol. 1, Taewon Publishing Company, Korea, 1974.

TRADITIONAL KOREAN CUISINE, by Woul Young Chu, Jai Min Chang, L.A. Korea Times, 1985

TRADITIONAL KOREAN MUSIC, edited by the Korean National Commission for UNESCO, The si-sa-yong-o-sa Publishers, Inc., Korea Pace International Research, Inc., U.S.A., 1983

TRADITIONAL KOREA - THEORY AND PRACTICE, edited by Andrew C. Nahm, Center for Korean Studies, Western Michigan University, 1974

TRADITIONAL THOUGHTS AND PRACTICES IN KOREA, Eui Young Yu and Earl H. Phillips, editors, Center for Korean-American and Korean Studies, California State University, Los Angeles 1983